THE CHANGING FACE OF TIBET

Pradyumna P. Karan

THE CHANGING FACE OF TIBET

THE IMPACT OF CHINESE COMMUNIST
IDEOLOGY ON THE LANDSCAPE

The University Press of Kentucky

Frontispiece: Elementary school children, some of them
members of the Red Youths, playing below the Potala Palace,
Lhasa, in 1964. *Courtesy of Shadow Studio.*

ISBN: 0-8131-1318-0

Library of Congress Catalog Card Number: 74-18935

Copyright © 1976 by The University Press of Kentucky

A statewide cooperative scholarly publishing agency
serving Berea College, Centre College of Kentucky,
Eastern Kentucky University, Georgetown College,
Kentucky Historical Society, Kentucky State University,
Morehead State University, Murray State University,
Northern Kentucky State College, Transylvania University,
University of Kentucky, University of Louisville, and
Western Kentucky University.

Editorial and Sales Offices: Lexington, Kentucky 40506

CONTENTS

Illustrations follow pages 24 and 60.

MAPS

THIS volume evaluates the ways in which the particular configuration of Chinese communist ideological attitudes has been shaping spatial processes and structures in Tibet. It is concerned with basic questions in cultural geography: How has the doctrine of communism expressed itself in the geography of Tibet? How has it molded the visible and invisible features of the landscape? These questions are approached by interpreting and assessing the patterns of change in Tibet since the Chinese occupation of 1951. After a consideration of Tibet's past, major trends of change are briefly described, followed by a more detailed discussion of changes in political, economic, and cultural patterns under communist rule. Although communism in Tibet reveals itself in many geographic phenomena, the doctrine has achieved remarkable spatial expression in the pattern of economic development, and has been carried to extremes, both ideologically and materially, in the political and cultural spheres.

I have had the privilege of intimate association with Tibet and Tibetan-speaking peoples for over twenty-five years. Despite the secrecy imposed by the Chinese on significant data dealing with population, economy, and regional development in Tibet, I have attempted to provide a coherent account of the impact of communism on the plateau's socioeconomic and political setting by analyzing and evaluating a considerable quantity and variety of information, including official news releases, radio broadcasts, and the eyewitness reports of refugees.

Although some of the information used in this volume is precise and trustworthy while some is vague, the considerable variety of materials available has enabled me to piece together a general picture of the patterns of change in Tibet.

The official news releases of the Chinese government, including newspapers, journals, and books, constitute an important source of information. Of particular importance are the various series of translations of Chinese printed matter, speeches, and radio broadcasts available from the American consulate general in Hong Kong, the Joint Publications Research Service of the United States government, and the Monitoring Service of the British Broadcasting Corporation. Official publications, journals, and newspapers from India, the United States, the Soviet Union, Britain, and Nepal have also been invaluable sources of information on developments in Tibet.

These published materials were supplemented by a variety of unpublished maps, air photographs, and other documents revealing changing geographic patterns in Tibet. Additional data were gathered through interviews with Tibetan refugees in various countries. Although refugees are valuable in furnishing information on how the communist system is working in Tibet, they are a special group whose sour views contrast with the official claims of universal success and popular support for communist policies in Tibet. Despite the recent thaw in the United States' relations with China, no American reporter or academic has been allowed to visit Tibet to make an outside appraisal of developments. By evaluating accounts of changes from 1951 to 1973 from the various sources noted above and in the bibliography against the background of my own field observations in early 1950, I have been able to trace patterns of change in Tibet's economic, political, and cultural life.

Acknowledgments are due to Tibetans and Tibetan-speaking monks and scholars, merchants, peasants, and nomads whom I had the privilege of knowing during my

travels in their homeland and some as refugees in India, Sikkim, Bhutan, and Nepal. I am also indebted to Professor N. C. Sinha, the leading Tibetan scholar and former director of the Namgyal Institute of Tibetology at Gangtok, Sikkim, who has shared with me many of his original ideas on the genesis and growth of Tibetan culture. The section dealing with Mahayana Buddhism was originally prepared by Professor Sinha. I should like to express my gratitude also to James E. Queen and David Oakes for the preparation of the maps, and to Miss Helen Corman, Mrs. Judy Botts, and Miss Susan Hamilton, who devoted much time and patience to the typing of the manuscript.

I am aware that many specific items in this volume may disappoint the pro-Lamaist readers, while much may also displease the pro-Chinese critics of Lamaist Tibet. My purpose is not to exalt or denigrate either Lamaism or communism, but to present the changes that have occurred in Tibet since 1951 under the impact of Chinese communism.

The spellings of Tibetan personal and place names adopted in this book are phonetic renderings of standard Tibetan as spoken in the Lhasa region. In order to avoid confusing the general reader unfamiliar with the written language, the strict transliteration of Tibetan words used when writing for Tibetan specialists has been considered unnecessary.

INTRODUCTION

THE importance of basic human values in providing the framework for decisions concerning spatial organization is widely recognized by geographers. The few existing studies attempting to explain landscape in terms of values are, however, mostly specialized and of limited scope. Since research in the field was pursued for different ends the resulting works are heterogeneous in content, presentation, and spatial scale. Towards the beginning of the present century, Ellen Churchill Semple vigorously asserted that the development of the landscape could be interpreted as a consequence of the distinctive features of the environment.[1] During the 1920s and 1930s geographers retreated from environmentalism, and the dominant role of man in landscape modification became a major focus of geographic investigations. Stress was on the study of concrete mapable elements and the processes accounting for them. This intense focus on visible landscape led to an unfortunate neglect of such invisible elements as ideology. The "sequent occupance" approach did hold that motivations, attitudes, and skills could "explain" the succession of land uses within a region and elucidate present patterns in the organization of space. In recent years geographic studies have considered the cultural landscape as a reflection of the human value system and attitudes, and human imprints on the landscape have been regarded as elements providing insight into the thinking of a cultural group about its surroundings. For example, Lowenthal and Prince note the reflection of human attributes and attitudes in the English landscape, and Tuan has noted the role of human values to explain man's use of the environment.[2]

While many fresh insights have been gained regarding the role of ideology in the organization of space, an ap-

propriate theoretical model for investigating the impact of ideology on landscape is lacking. Such a model would include three main elements: 1) the ideology; 2) the physical environment, including human and natural resources; and 3) the observable spatial patterns.

For geographic purposes, ideology may be defined as an intellectual structure based on certain assumptions about the general nature of social reality and providing a coordinated set of ideas about man's place in the environment and the principles of social, economic, and political organization. From this definition, a statement of the model might be: Ideology provides the base for decisions which set in motion specific actions or processes responsible for use of the environment and its resources, creating distinctive spatial patterns of human occupancy and use. In addition it should be noted that the extent and nature of the impact of ideology are limited by a fourth element, the technology available, since technology determines what impact man is capable of making on the environment.

Usually ideology evolves gradually but it may be changed abruptly through occupation or conquest, or through internal change within a country. Both the slowly evolving ideology and the sudden introduction of a new ideology are exhibited in the case examined here—Tibet. The traditional Buddhist attitudes and values, which found spatial expression in the landscape of pre-1951 Tibet, evolved over

[1] Ellen Churchill Semple, *American History and Its Geographic Conditions* (Boston: Houghton Mifflin, 1904).
[2] David Lowenthal and Hugh C. Prince, "The English Landscape," *Geographical Review* 54 (1964): 309-46; idem, "English Landscape Tastes," *Geographical Review* 55 (1965): 186-222; Yi-Fu Tuan, *Topophilia: A Study of Environmental Perception, Attitudes, and Values* (Englewood Cliffs, N.J.: Prentice-Hall, 1974).

a period of several centuries. With the Chinese conquest of the plateau in 1950 and 1951, a revolutionary, alien ideology was introduced. Chinese communism has imposed a new culture and a new way of life on Tibet, with resulting changes in the physical as well as cultural landscape.

The Marxist-Maoist ideology introduced by the Chinese functions as a landscape-changing agent in a number of ways. First, it provides a new framework for initiating and interpreting temporal and spatial processes of change. Second, it implies that all economic, social, and organizational considerations must be subordinate to the Communist Party's conception of collective interest. For instance, the development strategy, which depends on psychological as well as social mobilization, requires individual austerity and places a low priority on the production of consumer goods. Finally, the communist ideology furnishes the Tibetan people with a new set of basic values by which the individual and the community are to judge all thought and behavior. It stresses individual self-sacrifice in order to achieve goals prescribed for society. The values are inculcated by emphasizing 1) the superiority of dialectical materialism over the metaphysical theology of traditional Tibet, 2) mass education to suppress old irrational practices which are deemed expensive in terms of resources and land use, and 3) class struggle to eliminate institutions such as the family and religion which may impart opposing values, and to release peasants from all forms of feudal bondage.

Pre-communist ideology in Tibet was not directed toward exploitation of hydroelectric power, coal, and other minerals necessary for modern economic development. It did not intend to conquer the obstacles and hindrances to modern development, such as the inaccessibility of immense areas of mountainous and arid terrain. To the Buddhists the Tibetan landscape possessed supernatural significance, and economic activities such as farming served not only as a means of subsistence but as a form of participation in religious life. In contrast, the Communist Chinese view the landscape and its resources as elements to be manipulated in the quest for economic development. The cultural

landscapes created under the impulse of the two ideologies, then, differ not only in content and form but in meaning as well.

Although there is some disagreement among Marxists as to the relationship between man and his environment, communism maintains that a socialist society in which all productivity is planned, coordinated, and controlled by the state can have a major impact upon the natural environment.[3] Marxist ideology holds that without socialist enthusiasm, man in a feudal or capitalistic society tends to take the line of least resistance, abandons the struggle, and conforms as best as he can to the necessities of his situation, remaining forever backward. In the Communist Chinese view such appeared to be the destiny of Tibet under the rule of the Dalai Lamas.

Marxism, promising that man, suitably organized, could triumph over the natural environment, discards both the "determinist" school which maintains that man's progress is determined by the natural environment that surrounds him, and the "possibilists" school which maintains that the environment allows him various possibilities from which he can choose. Determinism is rejected on the ground that society evolves according to its own laws, and possibilism is discarded because the form of society, not choice, decides how far man makes use of the opportunities found in the natural environment.

One of the major landscape-transforming effects of Marxism in Tibet has resulted from its concern with the location of economic activity. Both Marx and Mao condemn economic specialization based on the exploitation of backward areas by the more advanced regions, and favor balanced economic development. One aim of the Chinese Communist regime in Tibet has been a diversified socialist economy aiming at self-sufficiency, with industries located close to

[3] I. M. Matley, "The Marxist Approach to the Geographical Environment," *Annals of the Association of American Geographers* 56, no. 1 (1966): 97-111; and J. E. Chappell, "Marxism and Environmentalism," *Annals of the Association of American Geographers* 57 (1967): 203-07.

sources of raw material and energy, and full development of the plateau's agricultural potential. The locational pattern of economic activity resulting from this policy has had an obvious impact on the plateau's geography and landscape. It has resulted in the many-sided development of the plateau, including establishment of industrial areas, an entirely new element in the Tibetan landscape.

Chinese communism has expressed itself in many ways in Tibet, but four areas—political patterns, economic activities, settlement patterns, and religion and education—in which it is written large across the Tibetan landscape, are discussed in some detail in this volume. The political organization of Tibet today, characterized by the concentration of authority among the centralized "revolutionary committees" dominated by Han groups in each of the sub-province level districts and counties, is a reflection of the ideologically based policy designed to bring about complete political integration of Tibet into the People's Republic of China. Communist ideology is clearly evident in the col-lectivist model of economic development. By 1970 the communes in Tibet were managing farming, distributing food and consumer goods, running industrial plants and educational systems, and sponsoring militia. The intensive development of new roads and communication networks was designed to integrate Tibet into the ideological structure of the People's Republic. The settlement pattern, comprising the groupings of production teams in each commune, represents the communist urge toward spatial agglomeration of habitat. The layout of roads and houses and the location of service centers also reveal the impact of ideology on landscape. The obliteration of organized religion and the new secular structure of the Tibetan educational system infused with Marxist-Maoist philosophy have had a profound impact on the plateau.

By 1974 Tibet had been transformed from a theocratic state to a communist state. Here is a good example of how the imposition of a new ideology can rapidly change the traditional cultural landscape of a country.

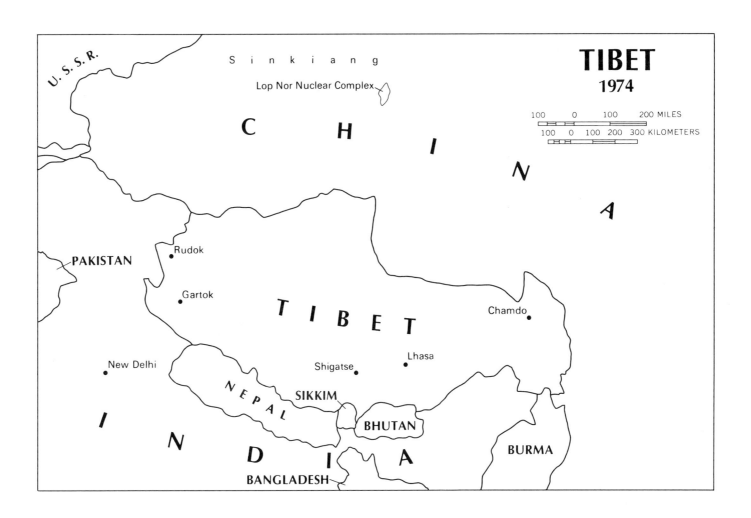

TIBET
1974

U.S.S.R.

S i n k i a n g

Lop Nor Nuclear Complex

100   0   100   200 MILES
100 0 100 200 300 KILOMETERS

C   H   I   N   A

PAKISTAN

•Rudok

•Gartok

T   I   B   E   T

Chamdo•

New Delhi•

Shigatse•

Lhasa•

N E P A L

SIKKIM

BHUTAN

I
N
D   I   A

BURMA

BANGLADESH

I

THE LAND OF TIBET

TIBET is one of the world's most fascinating countries, both culturally and physically. Isolated by terrain and determined to remain a stronghold of Buddhist faith, Tibet remained for centuries the most secluded and inaccessible country in the world. Within political Tibet[1] its priest kings established and maintained a system of government intended to preserve, defend, and foster the development of a distinctive body of Lamaist traditions and institutions, which constituted the *raison d'être*[2] of the Tibetan state and commanded the loyalty of its people. Almost forgotten by the rest of the world during most of its history, Tibet made headlines in 1950 when Chinese Communist leader Mao Tse-tung announced plans to "liberate" the Tibetan people. The communist occupation and the capitulation of Tibet in 1951, and in 1959 the uprising against the Chinese and the flight of the Dalai Lama to India focused the imagination and thoughts of millions around the world upon this sequestered land.

In 1951 the ideas, values, attitudes, and goals of Chinese communism replaced the well-being of religion as the basis for economic and political decisions affecting the organization of space in Tibet. The role of Chinese communism in the development of the contemporary cultural landscape of Tibet, and the visual as well as intellectual manifestations of communist ideology which have modified the human geography of the plateau are considered in subsequent chapters of this book. This chapter provides a background against which the reader may judge the changes that have come about in Tibet's political organizations and viability under communist rule.

Geographic Patterns

The boundaries of the Tibetan plateau, twice as large as Texas and delineated by the high peaks of the Kunlun and Himalayan ranges, are shared with the Chinese provinces of Sinkiang, Szechwan, and Tsinghai (Chinghai), and with India, Nepal, Sikkim, and Bhutan. Within its area of about 500,000 square miles, Tibet presents a pattern of extraordinary and striking physical landscapes.[3]

---

[1] Tibetan scholars distinguish three Tibets: the geographical, the cultural or ethnographic, and the political. Geographical Tibet includes parts of Sinkiang and areas which have since 1928 formed the provinces of Tsinghai (Chinghai) and Sikang. The people of Tibet have regarded Tsinghai and Sikang as part of their homeland. Cultural or ethnographic Tibet comprises all areas which were at one time inhabited exclusively or predominantly by people of Tibetan extraction. Political Tibet embraces only that part of geographical and cultural Tibet ruled by the Tibetan government from earliest times to 1951. For brief periods between the fourth and ninth centuries A.D., the political authority of Tibet extended from northern Burma to Afghanistan, and from Siberia to well inside present-day China. See H. E. Richardson, *A Short History of Tibet* (New York: Dutton, 1962), pp. 1-2.

[2] See Richard Hartshorne, "The Concepts of 'Raison d'Etre' and 'Maturity of States,'" *Annals of the Association of American Geographers* 30 (1940): 59-60; and idem, "The Functional Approach in Political Geography," ibid., 40 (1950): 95-130.

[3] David Snellgrove and H. E. Richardson, *A Cultural History of Tibet* (London: Weidenfeld and Nicolson, 1968), pp. 19-20, give three physical divisions: virtually uninhabited northern Tibet, comprising three-sevenths of the country; highlands and plateau areas of the south

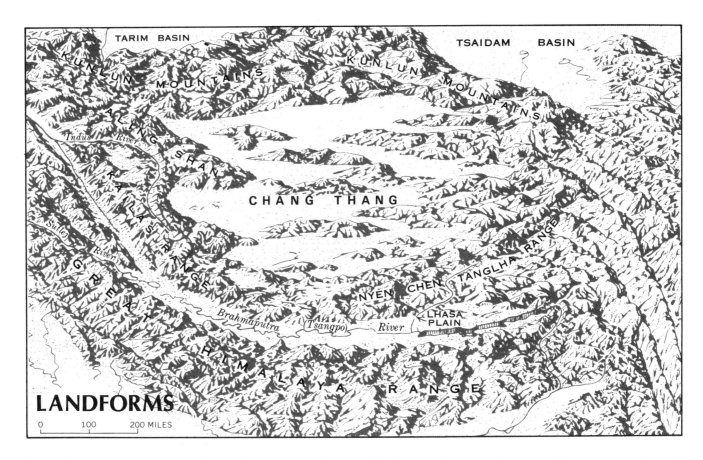

LANDFORMS

0   100   200 MILES

The northern part of Tibet, made up largely of a rocky desert plain called Chang Thang, covers nearly half of the country. A barren area characterized by intense continentality and aridity, it seldom receives more than one inch of rainfall annually. Although Chang Thang lies above 15,000 feet, snow seldom falls. The region is interspersed with numerous brackish lakes. Over this bleak plain the air is so rarified that the traveler can see an occasional nomad ten miles distant. Vast borax fields and dry salt lakes dot the landscape. Spaced far apart in the sparse grazing lands of the southern part of Chang Thang are the nomad tents, guarded against wolves and leopards by huge mastiffs. This

desolate region contains no settlements or towns of any size. Yet, by a kind of administrative miracle, officials always

inhabited by "small and scattered groups of nomadic herdsmen," forming two-sevenths; and "the extensive valley system of the Tsangpo and the Valleys of the Salween, the Mekong and the Yangtse," forming the remaining two-sevenths of the country. Owen Lattimore, *Inner Asian Frontiers* (New York, 1951), p. 207, divides Tibet from the viewpoint of human habitation into two areas: the center "a land of great height and the periphery of the central mass where the streams break down from the upper levels." George Cressey, *Asia's Lands and Peoples* (New York, 1950), p. 160, lists seven physical divisions: the Himalayan ranges in the south; the Karakoram in the west; the Tsangpo Valley; the Chang Thang plateau; the Altyn Tagh and the Kunlun in the north; the Tsaidam and Koko Nor basins; and Kham in the east.

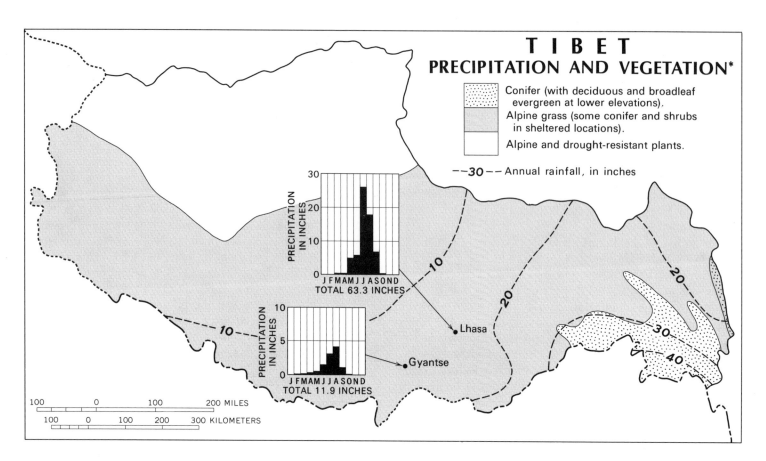

TIBET
PRECIPITATION AND VEGETATION*

Conifer (with deciduous and broadleaf evergreen at lower elevations).

Alpine grass (some conifer and shrubs in sheltered locations).

Alpine and drought-resistant plants.

--30-- Annual rainfall, in inches

PRECIPITATION IN INCHES
30
20
10
0
J F M A M J J A S O N D
TOTAL 63.3 INCHES

PRECIPITATION IN INCHES
10
5
0
J F M A M J J A S O N D
TOTAL 11.9 INCHES

Lhasa

Gyantse

100   0   100   200 MILES
100   0   100   200   300 KILOMETERS

reached the lonely black tents of the nomadic herdsmen to collect taxes and, more miraculously still, the nomads paid what they owed. By Tibetan standards, the scattered nomads of southern Chang Thang prospered, mainly from the export of wool to India. Almost 100,000 bales a year were shipped by caravan prior to 1951.[4] In addition, thousands of sheep carried tiny loads of salt, no more than thirty pounds each. The salt traffic moved year round. There was also a lively trade in yak tails, used as ritual fans in Hindu temples in India and for Santa Claus beards in Europe.

In contrast with Chang Thang, the long lowland valleys of southern Tibet, lying between 10,000 and 12,000 feet above sea level, contain fertile agricultural areas and the bulk of the nation's population. Except for a small area lying in the catchment of the upper Sutlej River, the drainage of southern Tibet escapes into the Tsangpo (Brahmaputra) and Indus rivers at the extremities of the Himalayan range. In the lower course of the Tsangpo the width of the valley floor is as great as ten to twenty kilometers.

The majority of Tibet's estimated three million people live in the southern valleys. All the principal cities—Lhasa,

* Based on data obtained from the Indian Meteorological Department.
[4] Based on estimates I obtained in 1961 from Indian traders in Himachal Pradesh, India.

Shigatse, and Gyantse—lie in this second major geographical division of the country. In the southern valleys the summer is warm but short. Temperatures rarely rise above 80° F., providing suitable growing conditions for barley, wheat, potatoes, peas, turnips, and apples. The climate of Lhasa (elevation approximately 12,000 feet) is characterized by a mean January temperature of 32° F., a mean June temperature of 63° F., and a frost-free period averaging 140 days. The coldest day of the year in Lhasa is generally 3° to 5° above zero. The rainfall associated with the moist monsoon winds from May to September varies widely. The average rainfall in Lhasa is about 18 inches, although 198 inches were recorded in 1936.[5]

The valleys of the Tsangpo and its tributaries, the Yarlung and Kyi Chu, comprise the most productive agricultural land in Tibet. The extensive valleys of southern Tibet are the result of erosional work by the Tsangpo and its tributaries which have cut through the rock strata overlying the granitic core of the Himalayas. The granite forms conspicuous outcrops in the valleys of the Tsangpo and Kyi Chu as well as in the immediate vicinity of Lhasa.[6]

Kyi Chu lowland, including the adjacent valleys of the Tsangpo and the Yarlung, was referred to as Ù or dBus in traditional Tibet.[7] Partially protected by mountain ranges, it formed a defensible area and served as the traditional cultural focus and center of political integration. Rival clans of nomadic non-Han tribes made their way from Central Asia to this region many centuries before the Christian era. Gradually they became sedentary and the stronger chiefs, after defeating their less vigorous rivals, made Yarlung Valley the focus of the region[8] and the official seat of their government. Later the capital was moved to Lhasa. Although the political limits of Ù fluctuated, throughout most of Tibet's history it essentially formed the strategic area along the Kyi Chu from Lhasa downstream to the Tsangpo and southeastwards to the Yarlung Valley.

Although Lhasa is not central in Tibet, its location combines two salient features.[9] First, its focal position at the site of the crossing of land and water routes gave the city a dominant position in Tibet. Second, the mountains surrounding the arable area around Lhasa provided marked military barriers, giving repeated pause to enemies coming from the northeast and northwest. From the Ù region, the early Tibetan state expanded along the Tsangpo eastward to the Dwagpo, Kongpo, and Poyul regions; westward to Tsang; and to Purang and Ngaris on the Upper Indus. The far-flung northern territory of Chang Thang was only gradually brought under the aegis of Lhasa.

A third swath of Tibet made distinctive by geography and climate is the eastern part, comprising the territory of Kham. This subtropical mountainous area covered with forests of oak and pine is drained by the Yangtze, Mekong, and Salween rivers. These three major rivers of Asia converge in eastern Tibet as if they were about to unite, but instead run parallel for about 170 miles in a narrow zone 50 miles wide, then suddenly diverge. "The parallelism and proximity of the Yangtze, the Mekong and the Salween in their exits from Tibet are amongst the most extraordinary features of the earth's land surface."[10] Chamdo, located on the Mekong River, has functioned as the regional capital of Kham.

[5] George B. Cressey, *Land of the 500 Million* (New York: McGraw Hill, 1955), p. 341.
[6] For details of geological structure see H. H. Hayden, "The Geology of the Provinces of Tsang and Ù in Central Tibet," *Memoirs of the Geological Survey of India* 36, part 2 (1907).
[7] For a discussion of the administrative areas of Tibet see Ram Rahul, *The Government and Politics of Tibet* (Delhi: Vikas Publications, 1969), pp. 37-39.
[8] For the origin of the Tibetan people see David Snellgrove and H. E. Richardson, *A Cultural History of Tibet* (New York: Praeger, 1968), pp. 21-22.
[9] See F. S. Chapman, "Lhasa in 1937," *Geographical Journal* 91 (June 1938): 497-507.
[10] Various explanations have been put forward to account for the parallelism of these great rivers. Lee has attributed it to parallel consequent drainage following sag lines on a fluted surface of warping. Some have regarded it as a result of alpine folding connected with the Himalayan revolution. Others have suggested the development of channels along parallel belts of weak rocks on a peneplain truncating folded structures. Rifting along fault lines has also been advocated as the cause of parallel depressions which became natural spillways for melt water from the Tibetan glaciers. See S. G. Burrard and H. H. Hayden, *The Geography and Geology of the Himalayas* (Delhi, 1908),

The history of this huge isolated mountainous territory is marked by a series of feuds and forays among the Khampa tribes.[11] Forgetting their internal feuds, however, the Khampas have united to fight the Chinese whenever they have attempted to establish their rule in Kham. Provoked by the Chinese in 1918, the Khampas threatened to invade the Szechwan plain, but the invasion was prevented with the assistance of Britain, which helped arrange an armistice. The armistice agreement divided Kham into two areas—the region west of the Yangtze River remained under the Lhasa administration with headquarters at Chamdo, while the region between the east bank of the Yangtze and the trading town of Kangting was constituted as an independent demilitarized zone under nominal Chinese administration. In 1928 and again in 1932 Khampas and Chinese Szechwan warlords were involved in bitter fighting until the Chinese were pushed back beyond Kangting into Szechwan.

After the death of the powerful Thirteenth Dalai Lama in 1933, the Khampas tried to drive even the Lhasa administration out of Chamdo. They also fought the Nationalist Chinese and Mao's retreating communist force which trekked through eastern Kham during the "Long March," October 1934 to October 1935. Despite the Khampas' efforts, between 1933 and 1949 the town of Chamdo and the entire area west of the Yangtze remained under the rule of governors appointed by Lhasa, and the border town of Kangting continued under Chinese rule. The influence and power of the Chinese governor extended only to the outskirts of the town, however. The rest of Kham was ruled by local feudal lords, such as the abbot of Litang, the chief of Batang, the princes of Dergue, and others. After the communist occupation of Kham in November 1950, the Chinese colonization scheme drove many Khampas from their homes and the Khampa guerrilla warfare presented serious problems for the Chinese authority throughout eastern and central Tibet.

The Spatial Growth of the Tibetan State

The origin of the Tibetan state is traced to the germinal core area[12] of the Yarlung Valley, about fifty miles southeast of Lhasa. (See back endpaper map.) The first Tibetan state had its center in this area when a Yarlung chief successfully brought rival chiefs and nobles of central and southern Tibet under his hegemony in the fifth century A.D. Along with the Lhasa region, this part of Tibet has been of great political and economic importance throughout history. It formed the base for continued accretions of territory and the dissemination of national feeling. The greater productivity and population of this core area were reflected in the location of estates and monasteries.[13] The fertile soil of the Kyi Chu Valley, producing crops within the limits of contemporary technology, and a population cluster large enough to exploit local resources and engage in long-distance commerce, furnished the economic base for spatial expansion of the state.

During the seventh and eighth centuries, the Yarlung kings maintained constant pressure on the northern and western borderlands of China in Kansu, Szechwan, Yunnan, and Shansi. It is remarkable that the economic and political power of the Yarlung kings, largely based on the productivity of the Tsangpo Valley and pastoral activities in the surrounding mountains, could support large and difficult mil-

---

p. 127; C. Y. Lee, "Development of the Upper Yangtze Valley," *Bulletin of the Geological Society of China* 13 (1933): 113; Arnold Heim and K. Krejei-Graft, "Szechuan-Tibet Expedition," *Zeitschrift Gesellschaft für Erdkunde zu Berlin* (1930), p. 269; W. Credner, "Observations on Geology and Morphology of Yunnan," *Liang-Kwang Ti-chin Tiao-cha-so* [Kwantung, Geological Survey], Special Publication 10 (Canton, 1932), p. 8; J. Coggin Brown, "Contributions to the Geology of the Province of Yunnan," *Records of the Geological Survey of India* 44 (1914): 98.

[11] Richardson, *Short History*, p. 11.

[12] For a concept of the core area and its applicability to the structure of political areas, see Roger E. Kasperson and Julian V. Minghi, eds., *The Structure of Political Geography* (Chicago: Aldine, 1969), pp. 75-76.

[13] For a partial list of these estates see Pedro Carrasco, *Land and Polity in Tibet* (Seattle: University of Washington Press, 1959).

itary actions both in Central Asia, from Turkestan and Kashmir to Nepal, and in western China. A unified Tibet extending well beyond the present political limits of the country, with Lhasa as the focal point, existed until 842 A.D., when the Tibetan state broke up into a number of political units, marking the end of the era of expansion in Central Asia. (See map showing the historical evolution of Tibet, front endpaper.)

For nearly four centuries thereafter, Tibet remained divided into a large number of petty states, each ruled by a local chief or nobleman. Armed warfare and rivalry between the great Buddhist monastic orders (Sakya, Kargyupa, and Karmapa) marked this period of political fragmentation. Local rulers were closely connected with the monasteries which they supported. The most powerful Buddhist sect in Tibet at this time was Sakya. In 1260 Kublai Khan, the Mongol (Yuan) emperor of China, recognized the grand lama of the Sakya monastery as the ruler of Tibet. During the period of Sakya dominance (1200–1350) the rich productive belt extending from Lhasa to Shigatse and Yarlung remained the core area.

The territorially-reunited Tibet under the Sakya grand lamas (who were under Mongol overlordship) was reorganized administratively and surveyed for taxation. A more efficient communication system comprising staging posts was established to weld the political territory together. Not until the rule of the Fifth Dalai Lama (1642–1682), however, was a high degree of administrative centralization achieved. The effective territorial control of the Sakya grand lamas, despite recognition by the Mongols, did not extend over all of Tibet. De facto political fragmentation continued. In the absence of effective central authority, the domain of each local ruler remained a separate territory for practical purposes. Nevertheless, the period of Sakya dominance marked the beginning of monastic hierarchs as rulers of the Tibetan state.

The collapse of the Mongol rule in China in 1368 also led to the decline in power of the Sakya grand lamas. Under the leadership of a Yarlung nobleman, the Sakya sect was

removed from power in the fourteenth century and Tibet again fragmented into several domains, but remained free of the political authority of the Ming (Han) rulers who succeeded the Mongols.

Toward the end of the fourteenth century, a powerful Buddhist sect, the Gelugpa, popularly called the Yellow Hat, came into being. It gained the support of several local rulers in the Tsangpo Valley, particularly in the province of Ü, and the powerful Mongol chiefs on the northern frontiers. In 1642 Gushri Khan, a Mongol chief, helped the Fifth Dalai Lama to subjugate petty rulers and established him as the undisputed sovereign ruler of Tibet.

During the reign of the Fifth Dalai Lama the territory of Tibet was welded together and districts ruled by native chiefs were brought under his control. Many monasteries, symbols of the new central power, were erected on commanding hilltop positions. These included the impressive Potala Palace, dominating the landscape of Lhasa, which continued to serve as the political center of Tibet until 1951. During his visit to Peking in 1653, the Fifth Dalai Lama was received as an independent sovereign by the Manchu ruler.[14] His death in 1682 resulted in a series of intrigues culminating in Chinese intervention in Tibetan affairs. Between 1720 and 1792 the Chinese gradually established domination over Tibet.

During the Manchu overlordship (1720–1911), the government remained in the hands of Tibetans with a loose system of Chinese supervision at the top exercised through the Manchu imperial representatives (ambans) at Lhasa. Reforms and administrative reorganization introduced during this period strengthened the power of the central government and brought all the territorial chiefs under the control of Lhasa. The productive land of the Tsangpo Valley continued to supply the economic base of power for the Tibetan rulers. Smaller states on the fringes of Tibet, however, such as Ladakh, Sikkim, and Bhutan, which at

[14] For different interpretations of this visit see Richardson, *Short History*, pp. 44-45.

various times had been politically linked with Lhasa, separated to become distinct political units.

In the nineteenth century Chinese power weakened in Tibet. In 1856, when Nepal imposed a treaty on Tibet securing extraterritorial rights and an annual tribute of ten thousand rupees, China was unable to protect Tibet. In 1890, after a military clash between Britain and Tibet, China confirmed Britain's protectorate over Sikkim. The British in India were guided by a desire to secure a well-defined frontier with Tibet and to develop trading relations with the country. After several unsuccessful British missions in the nineteenth century, the Younghusband military expedition in 1904 succeeded in securing a treaty with Tibet regulating trade and international relations.[15] After the Chinese revolution of 1911 the last vestiges of Chinese power in Tibet were removed when a small number of Chinese troops stationed in Lhasa were disarmed and shipped back to China in 1912.[16]

In Tibet the desire for freedom developed almost exclusively in relatively small circles of politically conscious people: high lamas, noblemen, chiefs, and estate owners. These people resented their dependent status and desired freedom from Chinese control. But the great majority of the people were not directly concerned. There was no question of the right of the individual to civil liberty or to any form of legal protection from a powerful and dictatorial government.

When independence was reestablished in 1912, the nation-state idea was already well developed among the Tibetan elite. It remained to develop a strong sense of nationalism among the citizenry. Loyalty to the person of the Dalai Lama, which claimed the support of all Tibetans, was already a strong unifying force. This religious sentiment transcended all parochial, sectarian, and regional loyalties. Lhasa, surrounded by the three powerful monasteries of Sera, Ganden, and Drepung, together housing over 20,000 monks, continued to be the center of power in all internal and external matters. With the renewal of Tibetan independence in 1912, the Thirteenth Dalai Lama became the

first monastic hierarch to assume absolute control of the Tibetan government.[17] He attempted to modernize Tibet so that it could hold its own as a sovereign nation, although his changes in traditional policies met strong resistance from the monastic bureaucracy. In 1913 he concluded a treaty with Mongolia in which the two countries agreed to provide each other mutual aid in case of danger from foreign sources. (See Appendix A.) After his death in 1933, Tibet was ruled by a regent until 1950.

In 1939, the reincarnated Dalai Lama was discovered at the age of four by a search party near Kumbum, east of Lake Koko Nor in an ethnographically Tibetan area of western China.[18] On October 8, the boy was brought to Lhasa for installation as the Fourteenth Dalai Lama. He was invested with ruling powers in 1950, at the age of fifteen, when military action was launched by Communist China. Traditionally, the Dalai Lama waits for his eighteenth birthday before formally assuming power. By staging the investiture ceremony ahead of schedule Lhasa's theocrats seemed to prepare for the worst, bolstering the spiritual position of the Dalai Lama in case the Communists tried to install a rival on his throne or he should be forced into exile.

A review of the territorial evolution of Tibet reveals two spatial elements. First, the compact territory between Lhasa and Yarlung has tended to become politically unified and dominant. Second, territories to the northeast, northwest, and south of Lhasa have tended to assert their independence

[15] See Peter Fleming, *Bayonets to Lhasa: The First Full Account of the British Invasion of Tibet in 1904* (New York: Harper, 1961).

[16] See Richardson, *Short History*, p. 102.

[17] For a detailed study of the Thirteenth Dalai Lama, see Charles Bell, *The Portrait of the Dalai Lama* (London: Collins, 1946).

[18] The existence of the reincarnated Dalai Lama and his whereabouts had been indicated to the oracle of Samye monastery. When visited by the search party, disguised as traders, the boy reincarnation recognized their holy calling and distinguished between the status of the individuals in the party. The boy took hold of the rosary which had belonged to the late Dalai Lama. In a further test, when the Dalai Lama's rosary, small drum, and walking stick were offered him along with replicas, he chose which had been his own in his previous incarnation.

from the central government. The degree of territorial integration has varied with the strength of the central political authority. There have been several alternations between integration and disintegration. As discussed earlier, the first Tibetan kingdom broke up between 842 and 1100. The Mongols welded together various territories governed by petty native rulers under the Sakya grand lamas (1200–1350). This political and spatial unity broke down after 1350, and the country again disintegrated into a number of territorial units controlled by monastic chiefs who supported the lay rulers. Tibet was administratively and territorially integrated again in 1642 with the help of the Mongols when the Fifth Dalai Lama was declared ruler of Tibet. Under the monastic rule centered in the core area of Lhasa, nearly all of Tibet was knit together. The exceptions were the northeastern and eastern borderlands comprising eastern Kham and Koko Nor, ethnographically Tibetan, which have seldom remained for long periods under the firm political control of Lhasa.

In an analysis of modern Tibet as a functioning political area, based on the common loyalty to the Lamaist church and the Dalai Lama, it may be useful to indicate three aspects of the internal geographic pattern. The first is the differentiation between the total territory of Tibet and the effective territory. The total territory comprises the whole of the plateau within its political boundaries, while the effective national ecumene, that part of Tibet in which most of its inhabitants are concentrated, forms only a small part of the total territory. Large areas of Tibet are essentially unproductive and sparsely populated. Second, the pattern of distribution—areas of concentrated settlement separated by very thinly peopled areas through which communications have been difficult and costly in the past—has hindered political and economic integration. Before 1950 the widely separated Tibetan communities developed local consciousnesses that competed with the idea of an integrated nation state. Third, the position of the Lhasa core area in relation to the rest of the national territory and to links with foreign areas has been a vital element in Tibet's development. This compact region has been the key to the economic, cultural, and political geography of Tibet.

The economic and political development of Tibet exhibits broad historical similarities with developments in Europe. Between the fifth and ninth centuries A.D., both Tibet and Europe were characterized by the role of feudal monastic authorities. Their economies were dominated by broadly similar patterns of agriculture and land-holding systems, including the raising of sheep and cattle. In early Europe as well as in early Tibet doctrinaire religious practices exercised the major influence on the life of the people. In Europe, Christianity was propagated and firmly established through the patronage of local lords and the resolute endeavors of monasteries. In Tibet, Buddhism was securely rooted by royal patronage during the reign of King Song-tsen-gam-po (605–650) and in the following centuries monastic centers and native rulers helped propagate Buddhism.

Between the tenth and fifteenth centuries, cultural and social developments in Tibet paralleled developments in the European Middle Ages. The philosophical ideas, literature, music, and arts which may be traced back to Greece and Rome made a major impact on the culture and civilization of Europe. In Tibet this cultural impact came mainly from India. In both areas the great religions prospered and overwhelmed the masses. Hierarchs in both the organized Christian Church in Europe and Lamaist monasteries in Tibet played a major role in society and in the government of the two areas.

The Middle Ages in Europe were followed by the Renaissance, with a regeneration of new knowledge in all spheres of human activity. In Tibet no comparable renaissance occurred. The hierarchs of the Gelugpa sect, the Dalai Lamas, continued to maintain a monastic monarchical state from 1578 until the Chinese occupation of 1951.

Socioeconomic Conditions in Pre-1951 Tibet

Before the Chinese occupation of 1951, Tibet was a theocracy. Much of the land belonged to the monasteries.

There were several hundred of them, and the largest—Drepung, for example, with about 10,000 monks in permanent residence—were formidable seats of power. Some had their own arsenals and private armies, which were used to maintain order in the surrounding countryside and at times also to enforce the will of the ruling monks on the central government. The senior lamas[19] were regarded as living incarnations of minor spirits of Buddha. Several thousand young men entered monasteries each year. Most monastic orders were celibate, thereby contributing to Tibet's chronic surplus of women, in spite of which polyandry persisted among a small minority.

In addition to the ruling monks there were nearly 150 to 200 leading noble families whose sons, generation after generation, made careers of government administration. They received no salaries but instead were rewarded for their services to the state by grants of land and serfs to work the land. Class distinctions counted a great deal. The gulf between a nomad herding sheep on the endless wasteland of the north and a nobleman of Lhasa, born and trained to rule, was vast.

Until the Chinese invasion there were no schools for the populace. The only schooling available to a young man was in the monasteries. The Fourteenth Dalai Lama is a good example of the product of this system. Poorly educated by any Western standard, he nevertheless is a man of great natural dignity and precious wisdom. The influence of education on the masses was negligible; of the two special schools in Lhasa in 1950, one was wholly devoted to the teaching of monastic novices and the other to the training of lay government officials. One private school educated the children of the nobles. The curriculum of monastery schools throughout the country included only Lamaist dogma and ritual.

Reminders of the penetrating influence of religion on the daily life of the country stood at every mountain pass, in monuments of loosely-piled stones inscribed with the sacred formula of Lamaism, "Om Mani Padme Hum" ("Oh, Jewel in the Lotus! Amen!"). The colorful costumes of the monks could be seen everywhere along roads marked out by centuries of use by human feet and by the hooves of yaks, mules, and sturdy Tibetan ponies, but unmarked by wheels. The brightly painted walls of monasteries dominated the drab, mud-walled Tibetan settlements; the blatant colors of monastic banners, the gorgeous trappings and jewel-encrusted ornaments of the high Tibetan monks, all emphasized by contrast the dreary dress of the peasants who lived in filthy hovels and cultivated the terraced fields of barley, soybeans, garlic, and peas in the lush valleys, and of the herdsmen in yak-hide tents who tended yak and sheep on the higher slopes.

The staple diet of the Tibetans has for centuries consisted of *tsampa* (slightly roasted barley-meal cakes) and a concoction of tea, yak butter, and salt. Women, strangely comely despite their shapeless woolen cloaks, did most of the field work. On proper occasions the whole male populace performed dances, the women participating only as spectators. The most notable sounds of pre-1951 Tibet were the pipe of festive flutes, the beat of drums, and the authoritative notes of the massive shell-horns which called monks and nuns[20] to their duties.

Magicians and oracles preyed on the superstitions of the people, to whom every river, mountaintop, or waterfall was the abode of a particular devil which had to be regularly appeased or exorcised. Over this landscape hovered vultures waiting to be fed with the specially butchered flesh and crushed bones of the dead, for there were no cemeteries in this land dedicated to a belief in reincarnation.

By acceptance of only the physically perfect into monastic life, the monasteries and nunneries created, even in this land

[19] The word lama in Tibetan corresponds to the word guru in Sanskrit. Padmasambhava (750–800), known in Tibet as Guru Rimpoche, ordained the first lamas. As the term guru is reserved for the "perfect" teacher, the term lama has been used for a limited number of monks. The paramount position of the lama is conspicuously indicated in Tibetan canonical literature, liturgy, and iconography.

[20] Little information is available on nuns. For an account of a visit to a nunnery, see Harrison Forman, *Through Forbidden Tibet: An Adventure into the Unknown* (New York: Longmans, Green, 1935).

devoid of international economic ambition, an increasing manpower shortage which undermined the social structure. The lamas, who made up one-fifth of the total population, were of primary importance in every community. Not only were all priestly rites concentrated in their hands but they were the masters of arts and letters. And, since many monasteries included extensive trading houses, they handled much of the nation's internal and external commerce. About four-fifths of the Tibetan population worked to support the one-fifth concentrated in the monasteries.

While the fundamental dogma of Lamaism made no discrimination in favor of wealth and position, the fact remained that there was a great gulf between the two strata of society into which Tibetans were divided. There was a close community of spiritual and temporal interests among the monastic rulers, the wealthy landowners, and the merchants, on the one hand, and among the peasants and herdsmen, irrevocably tied to the feudal estates, on the other. Polygamy and polyandry operated side by side, the peasantry apparently content with an average of three husbands to each wife,[21] and the nobles and merchants each generally supporting three wives. Monogamy was upheld only in those monasteries housing the two minor sects, the Black Hatted Bon and the Buddhist Red Hats. Strict celibacy was maintained by the dominant sect, the Yellow Hatted Gelugpa.

Tibetan Buddhism, symbolized by the wheel of life, the ever-returning chance to improve one's being in a fresh incarnation, provides a distinctive approach to human existence and to the passage of time. As the wheel of life keeps turning, so mortal man exchanges one body for another. Only *nirvana*, the absorption into the divine, provides a merciful release from the cycle of rebirths. For this reason time is best applied in meditation and looking toward the ultimate release from existence. The impress of this religious teaching on Tibetan society and character was profound.

Despite Chinese insistence that Tibet has always been a part of China, Tibetan religion, customs, culture, and language are all distinctive, amply sustaining a claim to self-determination and independence. The aloofness that long made Tibet a land of mystery was a matter of deliberate policy. Over the centuries Tibetans learned that the best way to get along with their more powerful neighbors was to keep them at a distance. A case in point was the Tibetan attitude toward the development of mining. Although the plateau reportedly contains deposits of gold and other minerals, mining was discouraged by the pre-1951 government. The leading monks warned that digging for gold would arouse hostile spirits in the earth and bring earthquakes in retribution. In truth, however, mining was discouraged because Tibetan leaders feared the effects of a gold rush from their more powerful neighbors—Russia, China, and India—that might overrun the country.

Isolation meant backwardness in the middle of the twentieth century. Tibetans found it more convenient to wade through streams than to build bridges, and used flint to strike fire for the evening meal. Intelligent Tibetans acknowledged the need for reform but felt that it must be initiated by Tibetans themselves and that changes must be introduced gradually. In a country where time and distance were measured, until 1951, by the pace of the yak (two miles an hour), they submitted that progress could not be pushed, least of all by a foreign power.

21 See Prince Peter of Greece and Denmark, A *Study of Polyandry* (The Hague: Mouton, 1963).

2

THE CHINESE INVASION
OF TIBET

On the eve of the communist invasion in the autumn of 1950, Tibet was ruled by the fifteen-year-old Dalai Lama, revered as the fourteenth living incarnation of Buddha. Through a regent and a *kashag* (High Council), the Dalai Lama exerted absolute temporal and spiritual power throughout Tibet.[1] Members of the *kashag* included the army commander-in-chief, the senior nobles, and the senior lamas. Their decisions were irrevocable in the context of the 1950 socioeconomic and administrative conditions of Tibet. Tibetans lived in a kingdom of absolute monastic and secular feudalism, where time was still measured by the length of a day's march and where age-old customs dictated by the Buddhist faith controlled their lives. Mao found in this situation ample material for rationalizing the invasion.

The Tibetan campaign began in late 1949 with the drilling of Chinese troops in mountain warfare and of party commissars in the Tibetan language and customs. On October 7, 1950, the Chinese advance got under way toward the forbidding Tibetan plateau from Yaan, a town in Szechwan near Kangting on the border of Kham. In four days the invaders reached Ning-ching, where a Tibetan border regiment defected. The Chinese then headed for Chamdo, the regional capital about 400 miles northeast of Lhasa.

As the People's Liberation Army, headed by General Chang Kuo-hua, overran the eastern Tibetan borderlands, it discovered that members of a Buddhist sect had installed a boy reincarnation of the exiled Panchen Lama as their spiritual head. Using the Panchen Lama as a rallying force, the Chinese Communists inducted thousands of Sino-Tibetan malcontents into a pro-communist army, thus successfully exploiting the old rift between the Dalai Lama and the Panchen Lama. While the temporal powers of the Dalai Lama have not been in dispute for centuries, the spiritual devotion of Tibetans was for generations divided between the Dalai Lama and the Panchen Lama. The latter, as the living incarnation of the Buddhist Spirit of Boundless Light (Amitabha or O-pa-me), was the superior of a huge monastery at Shigatse, Tibet's second largest city. The division of loyalties developed into a personal rivalry in the early part of this century and had its climax in 1924 in the flight of the Panchen Lama to China, where he gradually assumed overall authority.

In the face of the threat from Communist China, the Dalai Lama mobilized what forces he had—estimated at 10,000 to 12,000 men—armed only with British rifles, a few out-of-date field guns, and fanatical courage.[2] This meager equipment, even in the light of past Chinese military

[1] For the administration of Tibet during 1933–1950, see Ram Rahul, *The Government and Politics of Tibet* (Delhi: Vikas Publications, 1969), pp. 73-86.
[2] See H. E. Richardson, *A Short History of Tibet* (New York: Dutton, 1962), p. 17; for details of military organization in Tibet, see Rahul, *Government and Politics*, pp. 68-70.

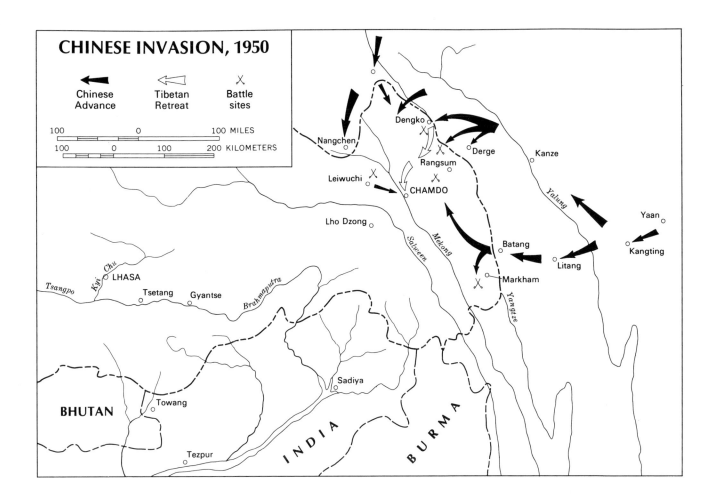

CHINESE INVASION, 1950

Chinese Advance | Tibetan Retreat | Battle sites

100   0   100 MILES

100   0   100   200 KILOMETERS

failures in the vast mountain wilderness which buttresses Lhasa, seemed hardly sufficient. With skillful handling, however, such a force could have done much to harass the invading Chinese in a terrain giving great advantage to the defense.

The Tibetan soldiers holding the vital frontier town of Chamdo were prepared for an orthodox daylight attack by the invading Chinese. Shortly after midnight on October 19, 1950, however, the garrison was awakened by the crash of explosions in the night air. Bright lights shredded the sky as Chinese troops, concealed outside the city, set off hundreds of rounds of rockets, star shells, and other pyrotechnics. Terror-stricken civilians ran through the streets. The cry went up that Chamdo was surrounded and resistance was useless. The Tibetan general galloped away to warn Lhasa of the danger, leaving his men behind. Within a few hours most of his men, their weapons scattered, followed him down the road to Lhasa. The next morning

abashed Tibetans remaining in Chamdo discovered that they had been routed by a fireworks display. Meanwhile, Chinese soldiers infiltrated the town and captured it without firing a shot. The bloodless Chinese conquest of eastern Tibet illustrated the ingenuity of the Communists in vanquishing the isolated, the timid, and the unwary.[3] As the Chinese pushed toward Lhasa, the Tibetan National Assembly sent an urgent appeal to the United Nations for help against the aggressors,[4] but the appeal went unanswered for lack of support from the governments of the United Kingdom and India.[5]

The Tibetan government, uncertain as to what the Dalai Lama should do, called the State Oracle, who was always consulted before making major decisions in times of emergency and distress. He urged flight. Before leaving Lhasa, the Dalai Lama was hastily invested with full power as ruler of Tibet, and the regency was abolished. In command of his country for the first time, just as it seemed on the point of dissolution, the Dalai Lama withdrew to Yatung near the Indian border but did not cross over.

While one group of Chinese forces was moving towards Lhasa from the east, a second group from Khotan, Sinkiang, crossed the Kunlun Range, trekked through the Aksai Chin region of India, and occupied undefended western Tibet.

From Chamdo on, the People's Liberation Army had no real opposition except from the rugged terrain. After a week's advance, the Chinese were reported a five days' march from the Tibetan capital. In Lhasa's golden-roofed lamaseries, the Buddhist theocrats spun their prayer wheels, consulted oracles, and conferred. The young Dalai Lama in Yatung had three courses open to him: flight across the southern border into India, diehard last-ditch resistance in Lhasa, or a deal with the communist invaders. Since it was now clear that no power on earth was interested in aiding Tibet, the Dalai Lama, convinced of the uselessness of resistance, sent a peace delegation to China in late December 1950.[6] In May 1951, a 17-Point Agreement was signed between the two nations. (See Appendix A.) The agreement brought to an end the Tibetan independence which had survived since 1912 without ever receiving de jure recognition. The 1951 treaty was the first agreement between Tibet and China after a lapse of 1130 years.[7]

The treaty provided for Tibet's ostensible self-government under the rule of the Dalai Lama, but gave China military control of the country and the exclusive right to conduct foreign relations. In view of the hold which the priesthood had on the Tibetan people, it was only prudent for the Chinese Communists to begin with a system of indirect rule and to work through existing institutions. The agreement, by guaranteeing the rights of the Panchen Lama and providing Chinese protection of him, tended to drive a wedge into the old order. Further, the agreement gave the Chinese wide scope for interfering in Tibetan administration to promote socioeconomic "reforms."

Returning to Lhasa in 1951, shortly after the signing of the agreement, the Dalai Lama received the Chinese emissaries. Much of what the Chinese proposed—schools, roads, hospitals, light industry—met with his approval. Many Tibetans welcomed the break with the feudal past. In 1954 the Dalai Lama made a six-months' visit to China and listened to lectures on Marxism, Leninism, and Maoism. Back in Tibet, Red technicians set to work. Several thousand Tibetan students were sent to schools in China. But from the start Chinese development plans and reforms held little appeal for the majority of Tibetans. The hard-driving communist cadres filled with Maoist zeal made little impression on the individualistic Tibetans, who felt that inner perfection of a man's soul was more important than an asphalt surface on a road. As the Khampa lands were collectivized and tribesmen were driven from their land,

[3] An account of the fall of Chamdo is given in Michel Peissel, *Cavaliers of Kham: The Secret War in Tibet* (London: Heinemann, 1972), pp. 40-43.

[4] United Nations Document A/1549, quoted in Bureau of the Dalai Lama, *Tibet in the United Nations* (New Delhi, 1961), p. 1.

[5] Richardson, *Short History*, pp. 185-86.

[6] Dalai Lama XIV, *My Land and My People: The Autobiography of His Holiness the Dalai Lama* (New York: Dutton, 1962), pp. 79-80.

[7] Richardson, *Short History*, p. 189. For a discussion of the international status of Tibet in 1950, see chapter 8, below.

and as monks and nobles lost power to commissars, the embittered Tibetans fought back. These events led to the uprising of 1959, which is considered later in this book.

What factors explain Communist China's overpowering desire to invade and occupy Tibet? The strategic value of Tibet has been pointed out as a principal reason. The economic resources of the plateau and the value of the area for colonization from the overpopulated eastern parts of China have been suggested as additional factors. The "return of Tibet to the Chinese Motherland," the commonly cited Chinese explanation, is hardly convincing. China is less the motherland of the Tibetans than England is the motherland of the Irish, for the Tibetans are quite distinct from the Chinese in language, religion, and culture.

The determination of the Chinese to use all available means to occupy and Sinicize Tibet is best explained by the Chinese perception of space surrounding their home-land. The Chinese view China proper as the center of the world, surrounded by a perceptual and conceptual organization of space in zones.[8] The value attached to each concentric zone in this spatial order decreases with the distance from the center.

One of the major aims of China's policy has been to secure physical domination of the territories which lie along its periphery. Since Tibet lies in this area it is thus regarded as an inseparable part of China which must be integrated into the national territory. Conceptually the territorial border conflicts between China and the Soviet Union and between China and India can also be explained in large part by the Chinese perception of space and the underlying cognitive values attached to this perception. The case of Tibet illustrates the importance of this spatial perception in determining Chinese foreign policy.

The minds of all patriotic Tibetans are haunted by the question of why Tibet fell. Certainly as a state Tibet was weak internally and materially. Except for a handfull of incarnations and aristocrats, few Tibetans would have affirmed in 1950 that their country had a perfect social order or a strong government.[9] At the end of World War II, with neighboring countries forging ahead in progress, Tibet was ripe for social changes and political reforms. The pronouncements of the Dalai Lama from his exile in India and the new constitution which he promulgated from Dharmsala on March 10, 1963, make it clear that the Tibetans aspire for a modern way of living and democratic reforms. They are not so much against socialism as against Han socialism. Since 1951 Tibet has been subjected to exploitation of resources and industrialization in the interests of the Hans.[10] Ideological and military goals dominate China's policies. The development of industries is intended to supply the needs of the large number of Chinese troops stationed on the plateau, and agricultural improvements have benefitted principally the Han settlers. Very little surplus is available for the Tibetan people.

As the Red cloud shrouds the plateau, many Tibetans concentrate on an integral precept of their faith which teaches that Gyalwa Chamba (the Loving One) will, at the chosen time, emerge from the west to save mankind. Expectant Tibetan eyes seem to be looking to the west for a sign, and some exiles lean towards the Soviet Union, viewing the Sino-Soviet dispute as hope for deliverance. In 1973 the Dalai Lama visited several European countries to help focus world attention on Tibet, and a pilgrimage to Buddhist sites in the Soviet Union was being planned in 1974.[11] In the meantime the plight of thousands of Tibetan exiles and the very existence of the exiled Dalai Lama serve as reminders to Asia and the rest of the world of Tibet's capitulation to China.

[8] Norton Ginsburg, "On the Chinese Perception of a World Order," in Tan Tang Tsou, ed., *China's Policies in Asia and America's Alternatives*, vol. 2 (Chicago: University of Chicago Press, 1968).

[9] B. Gould, "Tibet and Her Neighbours," *International Affairs* 26 (January 1950): 71-76.

[10] Henry S. Bradsher, "Tibet Struggles to Survive," *Foreign Affairs* 47 (July 1969): 750-62.

[11] "Diplomacy and the Dalai Lama," *Far Eastern Economic Review* 83, no. 11 (March 18, 1974): 22.

3

THE IMPRESS OF COMMUNISM
ON TIBET

GEOGRAPHERS have long recognized the major impress of cultural and political activities on landscape.[1] Today more than ever before technological capabilities have enabled man to imprint his ideological attitudes on the earth dramatically. The broad scope of governmental impress on the land and life of a political area is expressed through a variety of spatial distributions: patterns of resource exploitation, settlement and migration, levels of regional economic development, and special features such as military garrisons, which are symbols of the search for political security. The impact of some forms of governmental activity, such as the legal system or economic and political policy, is not directly visible but can be analyzed vividly in terms of the effects on spatial distributions.

In the developing world in particular, economic and social changes are diffused from selected nodes, usually major urban areas, along modern transport and communication networks. The diffusion of forces of change through governmental initiative is responsible for varying degrees of transformation in all areas of the developing world. New highways and automobiles alongside traditional trails and mule packs, and modern structures alongside old buildings characterize the dichotomized landscape resulting from the gradual diffusion of change.

To the geographer, Tibet is a unique and dramatic example of a major transformation of landscape and economy under the impetus of communist ideology. This ancient theocratic state, hidden in the vastness of Inner Asia and traditionally aloof from the politics of nations, was invaded in 1950 by the newly installed Chinese Communist regime and occupied in the name of Chinese sovereignty.[2] The Chinese occupation marked the beginning of revolutionary socioeconomic changes reflecting the communist doctrine in all aspects of Tibetan life. Here is a notable example of how the espousal of new political and social ideology can quickly change the face of an isolated, tradition-bound country. The transformation of Tibet under Chinese occupation since 1950 is unique not only for the speed of change but also for the fact that it has taken place in a difficult environment. It is an illustration of doctrinaire social and economic transformation executed by means of violent repression[3] of a peaceful and harmless people to achieve specific political goals.

[1] Derwent Whittlesey, "The Impress of Effective Central Authority upon the Landscape," *Annals of the Association of American Geographers* 25 (1935): 85-97; K. W. Robinson, "Political Influence in Australian Geography," *Pacific Viewpoint* 3 (1962): 21-24. For a recent study of the relationship between religion and landscape, see Karl B. Raitz, "Theology on the Landscape: A Comparison of Mormon and Amish-Mennonite Land Use," *Utah Historical Quarterly* 41, no. 1 (1973): 23-34.

[2] See chapter 8, below, for a discussion of Chinese claims to sovereignty over Tibet.

[3] See *The Human Cost of Communism in China*, report prepared

By the 1970s, with the complete elimination of traditional forms of government and other Tibetan institutions, the new social and economic doctrines of Chinese communism are strongly entrenched in Tibet, leaving a permanent mark on the land. The country has been transformed from a theocratic state into a major political-military bastion providing a base from which the Chinese can, if they choose, project power and influence into the bordering nations of the Indian subcontinent. Further, Tibet has become an important adjunct to the Chinese defensive posture in Sinkiang vis-à-vis the Soviet Union.

The political impress of Chinese communism on the Tibetan environment can be analyzed from two related perspectives. First, it can be analyzed in terms of communist political and military objectives. These objectives include territorial and cultural integration of Tibet with China, and "socialist" economic growth involving major state intervention in the harnessing of natural resources to support a regional military bastion. It can also be studied by examining the means, such as the successive programs of the communist governing bodies, by which communist political processes have manifested themselves. For example, the Preparatory Committee for the Autonomous Region of Tibet completely reorganized the administration of Tibet to bring it into line with forms obtaining elsewhere in China. Along with the destruction of the economic and political authority of the Tibetan monasteries, the socialist economic system, comprising extensive state regulation of the use and development of the physical environment, replaced the traditional Tibetan economic system in which basic spatial patterns were related to property ownership by the major monasteries and landlords. Restrictions on traditional trade with South Asian border countries, reorientation of the Tibetan economy towards China, maintenance of military garrisons at various centers to cope with internal security problems and to deal with possible hostilities against India, and development projects by the People's Liberation Army in Tibet exemplify a wide range of means by which the political impress has been etched on the landscape.

One of these processes of political impress can be seen in the political symbolism. Striking portraits of Chairman Mao and billboards displaying quotations from Mao's writings are highly visible in Tibetan cities, along major highways, at entrances to bridges, and at development project sites. Their presence is intended to impress on the Tibetans certain social and political values. In addition to dramatizing the success of Mao's political and economic path, their function includes achievement of the integration of Tibet with China.

While some of the effects of Chinese penetration are highly visible in the form of new highways, new construction associated with various development projects, and new political symbolism, other socioeconomic and political measures pursued during more than two decades have had an indirect impact on the landscape. It is possible to discuss the effects of certain aspects of socioeconomic and political measures in terms of their structural-functional attributes. For example, the traditional boundary of Tibet with the countries of South Asia was open for centuries with little barrier on the movement of people, goods, and ideas, other than that imposed by topography. The establishment of communist rule set in motion processes which led to the gradual tightening of the boundary, making it today one of the most impenetrable barriers in the world. As the outflow of Tibetan refugees across the boundary into South Asia became sufficiently large in the late 1950s and early 1960s to pose a threat to the economic development of Tibet and a source of embarrassment to the communist regime, the Chinese response was to increase the tempo and pattern of military fortifications and patrol along the border to stop the flow of refugees. By 1972, conditions of maximum security prevailed all along the southern Tibetan border. Trenches, bunkers, barracks, and ammunition storage in-

for the U. S. Senate Internal Security Sub-Committee of the Committee on the Judiciary, 92nd Congress (Washington, D.C., 1971). This publication estimates human casualties at between 500,000 and 1,000,000 of minority nationalities, including Tibetans, occasioned by the communist movement to "liberate" autonomous areas (p. 16).

stallations were the resultant pattern, symbolizing the determination of the Chinese regime to protect its economic and political position in Tibet.

The Chinese policy of encouraging the steady influx into Tibet of Han settlers,[4] whose numbers may someday simply inundate the indigenous population, is another factor which will eventually alter the face of the country. At the same time, by forcing most Tibetan monks and lamas to marry and moving them to China proper,[5] the old culture of Tibet is being eradicated. Restrictions of movement within, to, and from Tibet, have altered spatial linkages and earlier patterns of circulation.

The record of Han penetration and communist control in Tibet can be broken down roughly into five distinct phases. The first phase began in October 1950, with the Chinese army's successful "peaceful liberation" of Tibet, resulting in the formal agreement of May 1951. This initial phase culminated in 1954 with the Chinese in physical control of much of the Tibetan territory.

The second phase, which began in 1955 and lasted until 1959, marked the major extension of Chinese influence into the social, cultural, and religious aspects of Tibetan life. Through a comprehensive program of communist indoctrination and Sinicization, the traditional theocratic government of Tibet was transformed. Tibetan resistance and opposition to the integration of their country into the Han cultural world culminated in the general uprising of March 1959 and the flight of the Dalai Lama to exile in India.[6]

The third phase, from 1960 to the eve of the Cultural Revolution in 1966, was marked by abolition of the dual civil and religious governmental structure headed by the Dalai Lama, rapid obliteration of organized religion, intensification of the commune system, acceleration of economic development,[7] and a massive influx of Han into Tibet.

The period between 1966 and 1968, the years of the Cultural Revolution in Tibet,[8] comprises the fourth phase of Han penetration. It was characterized by the widespread destruction of relics of Lamaist Buddhism by the Red Guards, struggle among various Chinese revolutionary fac-

tions in Tibet, and some weakening of Chinese control, which encouraged Tibetan insurgency.

The current phase, which began in 1969 in the aftermath of the Cultural Revolution, is characterized by a new governmental structure which has institutionalized the outcome of the Cultural Revolution, and the accelerated development of Tibet as a military bastion. The period since 1969 has seen a continuation of the fighting between rival local factions long after order was restored in other areas of China. With continued subversion and sabotage by resistance groups, Tibet remains one of the most troubled regions under China's occupation.[9] It is a land which is being harshly modernized with strict adherence to the dominant communist value system at a great cost to its people.

1950–1954: *The Consolidation of Chinese Control*

In the treaty of May 1951, China pledged not to alter the established status, functions, or powers of the Dalai Lama.

[4] Only the Hans, who comprise the dominant ethnic group in China, have been sent to Tibet as settlers. Minority ethnic groups such as the Mongols, the Hui, the Manchus, and the Uighurs form only about 6 percent of China's population, but the territories in which they live constitute over half of China. Minority groups retain anti-Han prejudice to varying degrees. Historically, the Hans have perceived the ethnic minorities as primitive, less civilized people living on vast regions along the borders of China proper. Nearly 500,000 Hans were settled in Tibet during 1954-1956. After the 1959 uprising a rapid increase of Han settlers was reported. See *New York Times*, November 28, 1956, p. 7; April 5, 1959, p. 9.

[5] *New York Times*, July 18, 1956, p. 4; February 6, 1957, p. 10.

[6] For a detailed account of the seven weeks of anguish and violence during the seige and fall of Lhasa, see Noel Barber, *From the Land of Lost Content: The Dalai Lama's Fight for Tibet* (Boston: Houghton Mifflin, 1970); see also Verrier Elwin, "The Dalai Lama Comes to India," *Geographical Magazine* 32, no. 4 (1959): 161-69.

[7] P. H. M. Jones, "Tibet's Emerging Economy," *Far Eastern Economic Review* 31, no. 7 (February 16, 1961): 288-91.

[8] For a list of Red Guard publications which provide an account of the ideological battle and the forces dividing the Chinese in Tibet, see "The Cultural Revolution in Tibet," *Tibetan Review* 2, nos. 1-2 (1969): 15. A graphic account of rampage during the Cultural Revolution is "The Making of a Red Guard," *New York Times Magazine*, January 4, 1970, p. 84.

[9] *New York Times*, September 5, 1971, p. 8.

Although this pledge was observed on the surface at first with no formal attempt to alter the traditional institutions of Tibetan administration, China began to lay the groundwork for concerted action that was to transform Tibetan society. Soon after the signing of the treaty, China redefined the concept of local government as designated in the treaty, to regard Tibet not as a single political-territorial unit but as comprising three equal and independent units, each having a separate administration. These three units were the territory of central Tibet ruled by the Dalai Lama, the area around Shigatse administered by the Panchen Lama, and the strategic eastern area of Chamdo, which forms the gateway from China to Tibet. China then interpreted its pledge to maintain traditional Tibetan institutions to apply only to the territory of central Tibet around Lhasa ruled directly by the Dalai Lama. Reforms could then be initiated in the rest of the plateau with no obligation to seek approval from the Dalai Lama's government.

Although there is no historical basis for the partition of Tibet, China cogently used the lack of direct political control by the Dalai Lama outside the Lhasa area to advance its own control. The Chinese action giving equal status to the Chamdo and Shigatse areas was viewed with satisfaction by the warlike tribal inhabitants of Chamdo, who have been traditionally semi-independent of Lhasa; it was also enthusiastically greeted by the Panchen Lama, who was portrayed by China as sovereign within the Shigatse region. After effectively insulating both regions from the territorial authority of the Dalai Lama and breaking their traditional loose political links with Lhasa, China moved to consolidate its effective political control in both areas.

The Chamdo region was first singled out for close integration with China because of its strategic location. In early 1951, Chamdo became the seat of the newly formed People's Liberation Committee charged with administering the region. As the city in Tibet most accessible to China, Chamdo began to emerge as a major political administrative center. The Chinese began to move Tibetan offices to the city, and thus outside the influence of the Dalai Lama's

government. Although Nagbo Nawang Jigme,[10] a member of the Dalai Lama's cabinet, nominally headed the Chamdo government, the territory was brought under the effective rule of the local Chinese military authority. By early 1952 Chamdo was completely independent of Lhasa. As Han settlers began to arrive in Chamdo in the early 1950s, their encroachments on the customary territory of Tibetan tribes generated considerable hostility. The Khampas, a border tribe, revolted against the Chinese, and their defiance stood in the way of complete transformation of the region. With full military dominance, however, the Chinese wielded complete authority in Chamdo by 1954.

In the Shigatse area, China expanded its political control indirectly by securing the full loyalty of the Panchen Lama, by elevating him to parity with the Dalai Lama, and by exploiting the old hostility between the Panchen and Dalai and their respective entourages. Under the leadership of the Panchen Lama, the Shigatse region remained submissive and fell easily into China's political control. Because of the Panchen Lama's position as the head of vast land holdings in Shigatse having large serf populations, and because of his spiritual eminence as head of the Trashi-lhünpo monastery with its vast wealth and influence, the Dalai Lama's government had generally refrained from direct interference in the administration of territories under the jurisdiction of the Panchen, although it had maintained provincial governors at Shigatse who worked with the Panchen Lama. Historically, the Dalai Lama's political power and authority were regarded as paramount over all of Tibet, even though in reality his effective authority was circumscribed by the feudal political pattern in which large landed estates were held in fiefdom by the local lords, who acted as administrative heads of various areas. The Panchen Lama, who stood slightly above the Dalai Lama spiritually at the apex of the monastic hierarchy, was not secularly the equal of the Dalai. By treating the Panchen as sovereign within the

[10] Nagbo, a Tibetan, had served as the Dalai Lama's governor in the Chamdo region and as commander-in-chief of the Tibetan military units in eastern Tibet.

Shigatse area, the Chinese withdrew a part of Tibet from the Dalai Lama's secular control. They encouraged disgruntled feudals and nobles from Lhasa who were frustrated in their political ambitions, and other dissatisfied groups opposed to the Dalai Lama's government, to gather in Shigatse. Led by the Chinese, these diverse anti-Lhasa elements attempted to undermine the power and influence of the central regime.

In contrast to Chamdo and Shigatse, where China encountered little resistance, the traditionally strong Tibetan elements and institutions in the Lhasa region offered major obstacles to the expansion of Chinese domination and socialist transformation. China's policy was therefore aimed at weakening the internal unity of the established regime. Its tactics involved support of dissident elements whose agitation would diminish the political power of the Dalai Lama's government. The Chinese policy also called for downgrading the divinity of the Dalai Lama and undermining the awe and mystery surrounding his symbolic position as Tibet's god king. A major effort was made also to abolish the primacy of monks and to curtail the public and semiofficial privileges, prestige, and influence of the monasteries, major centers of conservatism.

Through education and by infiltration of social, religious, and cultural groups, the Chinese encouraged disenchantment among the Tibetan populace. Indoctrination in Marxist philosophy was carried on by social organizations such as the Tibetan branch of the New Democratic Youth Federation of China, formed in Lhasa in May 1952. To win favor with the masses of peasants, cattle-herders, and nomads, who toiled under oppressive burdens of feudal bondage, China pressed the local authorities to alleviate their economic conditions. The Chinese took full credit for the successful program of reducing accumulated grain and money debts and waiver of back interest, a program already being carried out by the Dalai Lama's government in 1953. The exploitation of the masses by the nobility, monasteries, and large landowners was used effectively to destroy the traditional cohesiveness of Tibetan society and polity. Further,

Chinese control over trade and commerce facilitated domination over the trading community. Road construction assisted integration with China, and the development of health facilities, such as the Lhasa People's Hospital, opened in 1952, was designed to gain the support of the local population. As agreed to in the 1951 treaty, the Tibetan armed forces were integrated into the Chinese army. The Tibetan Foreign Office[11] was closed and the diplomatic affairs of Tibet were taken over by China.

Despite these major Chinese efforts, the power, prestige, and privilege of the conservative Tibetan hierarchy remained supreme. China did, however, succeed in bringing about some structural and functional changes in the Dalai Lama's government, particularly in secularizing the administrative system. By the end of 1954, China had consolidated its physical hold in all areas of Tibet except the Lhasa region.

1955–1959: A New Political Structure and the Rise of Insurgency

In the 1951 Sino-Tibetan treaty, China recognized the distinctive status of Tibet as a "special" autonomous region. This special position was abolished, however, in 1954 when Tibet was declared an autonomous region of China similar in standing to other ethnically non-Han areas under the Constitution of the People's Republic of China. The concept of Tibetan nationhood which the Dalai Lama's government had always advanced received a major setback when the new constitution was endorsed by Tibetan delegates attending the legislative session in Peking in 1954. The political relations between China and Tibet were not to be governed now under the parainternational 1951 treaty, but under Chinese domestic law. Autonomous status was not bestowed immediately, however, because Chinese control was not yet fully secure, particularly in Lhasa.

A Preparatory Committee for the Formation of the

[11] The Tibetan Foreign Office was established by the Thirteenth Dalai Lama in 1926 to administer the expanding foreign relations, mainly with India, Nepal, and Mongolia.

Autonomous Region of Tibet was established in 1955. This body was made up of representatives of the Dalai Lama's government, the Panchen Lama's council, the People's Liberation Committee of the Chamdo area, major monasteries and other Tibetan organizations, and Chinese government personnel in Tibet. With the Dalai Lama as chairman, the Panchen Lama as vice-chairman, General Chang Kuo-hua as deputy, and Nagbo Nawang Jigme as the secretary-general, the committee was to function as the central administration of Tibet, deriving its authority from and dependent on the State Council of the People's Republic of China in all respects. The formal chairmanship of the committee by the Dalai Lama was no restraint on the Chinese because most Tibetans appointed to the committee were Chinese puppets. In any case, the major decisions were made by the Committee of the Chinese Communist Party in Tibet, on which Tibetans were not represented.[12]

The Preparatory Committee established several subordinate administrative agencies. Through these agencies dealing with civil administration, finance, health, the judiciary, agriculture, trade and industry, transportation, and construction, all dominated by Han personnel, China successfully wrested political power from Tibet's traditional leaders—a task in which they had not succeeded during the 1950–1954 period.

The initiation of large-scale secular education with a communist-oriented curriculum, the construction of hydroelectric stations, factories, experimental farms, and roads now began to have a major impact on the landscape of the country, its economy, and its people. The increasing Han control of Tibetan affairs also generated mounting unrest among the people. Embittered by Han management of their affairs[13] and the rapid development of local economic resources to strengthen China's position, groups of Tibetans reacted with armed uprisings at various places on the plateau in 1957. Nor did the withdrawal of some Han personnel[14] satisfy the Tibetans. To the continued uprisings in 1958 China responded by heightened repression. By early 1959,

the stage was set for a head-on collision between a China determined to gain political supremacy and the Dalai Lama's government, which sought desperately to preserve its traditional identity and institutions.

Mimang Tsongdu, a popular anti-Han protest movement, came into being in 1951. Lacking central direction, Mimang was not an organized political movement in the modern sense but a spontaneous movement largely based on anti-Chinese emotional ferment. As the Chinese grip tightened in the 1950s, the Mimang movement spread rapidly,[15] manifested in sporadic disruptions of communications and destruction of bridges.[16] These activities undoubtedly annoyed the Chinese but did not constitute a strong, well organized insurgency.

In early 1959, Mimang is estimated to have had over three hundred thousand supporters in Tibet and adjoining areas[17] and some members of the movement set forth several charges against the Chinese. These included: the taking of grain; destruction of thousands of acres of farmland "on the pretext that national highways and barracks and arsenals were to be built there"; seizure of land and its allocation to Chinese immigrants; slave labor; persecution of lamas and monks, many of whom were forced to marry; and forced indoctrination in communism, particularly of lamaist leaders. These charges were investigated and substantiated by a committee of the International Commission of Jurists.[18]

The growing influence of the Mimang movement and the opposition to modernizing the country along socialist lines

[12] Dalai Lama XIV, *My Land and My People: The Autobiography of His Holiness the Dalai Lama* (New York: Dutton, 1962), p. 133.

[13] *New York Times*, January 13, 1957, p. 1.

[14] Ibid., October 12, 1957, p. 2.

[15] Ibid., March 19, 1958, p. 16

[16] "Tibet under Communist Occupation," *World Today* 13 (July 1956): 293.

[17] A. H. Stanton Candlin, *Tibet at Bay* (New York: American-Asian Educational Exchange, 1971), p. 32.

[18] *The Tibet Revolution and the Free World* (Taipei: Asian People's Anti-Communist League, 1959), p. 21. International Commission of Jurists, *Tibet and the Chinese People's Republic* (Geneva, 1960).

Nagbo Nawang Jigme (left), Chu Teh, vice-chairman of the People's Government of China (right), and other Chinese officials toasting the "peaceful liberation of Tibet" during surrender ceremonies in 1951.

Courtesy of China Photo Service.

Chinese soldiers in front of the Potala Palace.

Courtesy of China Photo Service.

The Dalai Lama and Mao Tse-tung exchanging a
ceremonial scarf in Peking in 1954.

Courtesy of China Photo Service.

The Dalai Lama (left) and the
Panchen Lama in Peking in 1954.

Courtesy of China Photo Service.

The Panchen Lama being welcomed to Lhasa on April 5, 1959. At right is General Chang Kuo-hua, commander of the Tibet Military Region.

Courtesy of China Photo Service.

The Dalai Lama with Prime Minister Nehru in New Delhi in November 1956.

Courtesy of Press Information Bureau, Government of India.

The walled city of Gyantse, with its huge chorten Kumbum, one of the best known in Tibet.

Courtesy of East Photo, New York.

New buildings in Lhasa built by the Chinese during the 1960s, as viewed from Potala Hill.

Courtesy of China Photo Service.

Gelugpa monastery in Gartok. The temple is at center
and the monks' cells are within the walls.

Courtesy of Ewing Galloway.

Trucks moving along the Szechwan-Tibet highway
through Chamdo in eastern Tibet.

Courtesy of Economic Information & Agency, Hong Kong.

Modern vehicles moving past a cotton field. The highways leading into Tibet from Szechwan and Tsinghai have brought great changes along their routes.

Courtesy of Economic Information & Agency, Hong Kong.

Construction site of a hydroelectric power plant near Lhasa, 1959.

Courtesy of China Photo Service.

Sheepherding in central Tibet. Pastures around
the lake basins can be used year round.

Courtesy of China Photo Service.

Workers in a tomato field at the
Agricultural Experiment Farm near Lhasa.

Courtesy of China Photo Service.

Tibetan herders of the arid northwestern plateau.
Formerly nomadic, many have now been
settled in permanent dwellings.

Courtesy of G. R. Jani.

Chinese scientific workers camping on Central Rongbuk
Glacier, north of Mount Everest, at an
altitude of 18,700 feet.

Courtesy of Economic Information & Agency, Hong Kong.

led to the Lhasa uprising of March 1959.[19] Shortly before its outbreak rumors were circulating in Lhasa that China intended to depose or abduct the Dalai Lama. On March 12, in defiance of Chinese orders against carrying weapons, about ten thousand armed Tibetans marched on the Potala, the main palace of the Dalai Lama, and the Norbu Lingka, the summer palace, to protect their sovereign god king and to demonstrate against communist rule. The Khampas from the border regions, conservative elements within Lhasa, and native factions among the nearby monasteries led the insurgents. The confrontation remained highly localized in Lhasa and its environs. Although most Tibetans resented Han rule and its policy of socialist transformation, apathy, apprehension, traditional disinterest in politics, and aversion to violence prevented the leaders of the insurgents from mobilizing the entire population. Failure to forge a united front against the Chinese reduced the uprising to a mere gesture of defiance. The Khampas, a formidable element, carried out determined assaults on the Chinese garrisons and by March 12 the region south of Lhasa was in turmoil. As the Chinese moved heavy reinforcements into Lhasa demanding an end to the resistance, it was evident that a final struggle was about to begin which could well result in the capture of the Dalai Lama. At the urging of Tibetan leaders, the Dalai Lama escaped from Lhasa on the night of March 17 in the simple garb of a monk and sought asylum in India.

The Lhasa revolt was effectively suppressed by the People's Liberation Army, although sporadic guerrilla warfare continued. Considering the limited territorial extent of the conflict and the limited number of people and factions who took an active part in the hostilities, this cannot be called a national insurrection. Environmental difficulties and the lack of transport and communications prevented the uprising from spreading and assuming mass proportions. In a sense, however, the revolt may be considered national since it involved Lhasa—the seat of government and a symbol of the spirit of the Tibetan people.

With the collapse of the insurgency and the flight of the Dalai Lama to India, the way was paved for absolute Chinese control. In implementing its policies in Tibet, China would no longer have to consider the reaction of the Dalai Lama and his considerable influence over his people.

In September 1959, the Dalai Lama appealed to the Secretary General of the United Nations, requesting immediate consideration of the Tibetan issue by the General Assembly. Following an extensive debate, the General Assembly adopted a resolution on October 21, stating that the human rights of the Tibetan people had indeed been violated.[20] The resolution amounted to a vote of censure on China, but no action was taken to assist Tibet.

1960–1966: *Socialist Transformation*

The Han goal of molding Tibetan society and polity into the "socialist" image of the People's Republic of China was greatly facilitated by their triumph over the Lhasa insurrection. Immediately after the 1959 revolt, a decree of the State Council of the People's Republic of China dissolved the government formerly headed by the Dalai Lama.[21] At the same time the Preparatory Committee was made the principal instrument of Chinese rule with complete control of local administration. The Panchen Lama replaced the Dalai Lama as chairman. The reconstituted committee, with new members replacing the "traitorous elements," undertook the task of reorganizing the sociopolitical system. These moves marked the elimination of the last remnants of Tibetan autonomy and the establishment of a system of regional administration submissive to the People's Republic.

Major changes in the spatial organization of the administrative system eliminated the feudalistic land tenure and civil administration systems. Communist-indoctrinated Tibetan graduates of Nationalities Institutes were brought back

---

[19] For eye-witness accounts see "The Lhasa Uprising, March, 1959," *Tibetan Review* (Special Issue), 2, no. 3 (1969): 1-24.

[20] United Nations Documents A/4234, A/4848.

[21] For the text of the decree see *Concerning the Question of Tibet* (Peking: Foreign Languages Press, 1959), pp. 1-3. *New York Times*, March 29, 1959, p. 3.

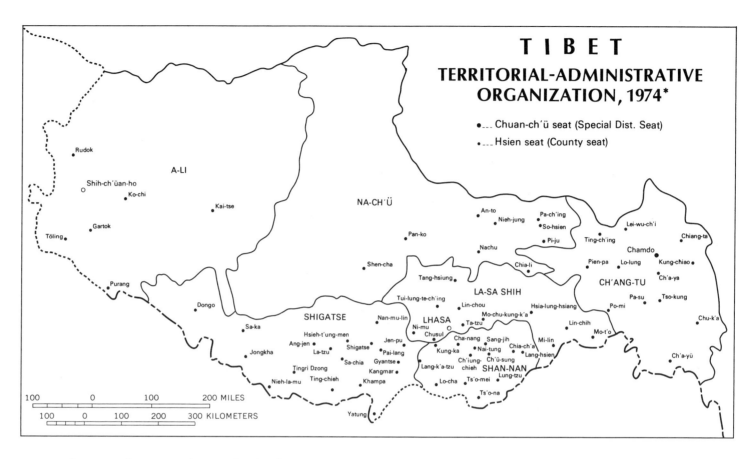

TIBET
TERRITORIAL-ADMINISTRATIVE
ORGANIZATION, 1974*

- •... Chuan-ch'ü seat (Special Dist. Seat)
- •... Hsien seat (County Seat)

Rudok

A-LI

Shih-ch'üan-ho
Ko-chi

Kai-tse

NA-CH'Ü

An-to
Nieh-jung
Pa-ch'ing
•So-hsien

Lei-wu-ch'i

Chiang-ta

Gartok

Töling

Pan-ko

Pi-ju
Nachu

Ting-ch'ing

Chamdo

Kung-chiao

Purang

Shen-cha

Chia-li

Pien-pa
Lo-lung

Ch'a-ya

CH'ANG-TU

Dongo

Tang-hsiung

LA-SA SHIH

Pa-su
Tso-kung

Tui-lung-te-ch'ing
Lin-chou

Hsia-lung-hsiang

Po-mi

SHIGATSE

Nan-mu-lin
LHASA

Ni-mu
Chusul

Ta-tzu

Mo-chu-kung-k'a

Lin-chih

Chu-k'a

Sa-ka

Hsieh-t'ung-men

Ang-jen
Jen-pu
Shigatse
Pai-lang

Cha-nang
Sang-jih
Nai-tung
Chia-ch'a
Mi-lin
Lang-hsien

Mo-t'o

Ch'a-yü

Jongkha
La-tzu
Sa-chia
Gyantse
Kung-ka

Ch'iung-
chieh
Ch'ü-sung

Tingri Dzong
Kangmar

Lang-k'a-tzu

SHAN-NAN

Nieh-la-mu
Ting-chieh
Khampa

Lo-cha
Ts'o-mei
Lung-tzu

Ts'o-na

Yatung

```
100       0       100     200 MILES
100   0   100   200   300 KILOMETERS
```

from China[22] and appointed to all levels of government.

In 1965, Tibet was divided into five "special districts," or *chuan-ch'ü*: Chamdo (Ch'ang-tu), Tse-tang (Shan-nan), Nagchu (Na-ch'ü), Shigatse (Jih-k'a-tse), and Ari (A-li), and the large *shih* (municipality) of Lhasa (La-sa). These divisions are shown on the map. These special districts and the *shih* were further subdivided into seventy *hsien* or county administrative units. The commune is now the basic sub-*hsien* political unit. Within each commune small production teams comprising several households in a village or a residential grouping within a village form the lowest administrative unit for political and economic purposes.

At the same time a major land redistribution program[23] was initiated, involving the breaking up of the big estates

* Due to frequent modifications in boundaries and lack of precise information, *hsien* boundaries are not shown. Dashed lines (···) indicate traditional boundaries such as the Tibet-Western India and Tibet-Bhutan boundaries; broken lines (·—·—) show international boundaries defined in treaties and in some areas demarcated on the ground, such as the Tibet-Nepal and Tibet-Burma boundaries defined in 1960, the Tibet-Sikkim in 1890, and the Tibet-Eastern India in 1914.

22 *Survey of China Mainland Press* (American Consulate General, Hong Kong), no. 2033 (June 19, 1959): 36; no. 2075 (August 13, 1959): 37.

23 For details of the "democratic reforms" and "redistribution of land," see *Current Background* (American Consulate General, Hong

formerly owned by the monasteries and nobility, and distribution of land to the peasantry. Farmers' cooperatives were established to pave the way for eventual collectivization of agriculture and the introduction of communes. Although major changes were accomplished in agriculture (see chapter 5, below), the vast pastoral areas of Tibet remained untouched by reforms. The Chinese concentrated their efforts on anchoring the pastoralists to permanent winter quarters to increase their control over this semi-nomadic population.

In the field of education, the role of the monasteries, the traditional centers of Tibetan learning, was eliminated, with complete control of administration by the Chinese. An accelerated program based on communist educational policies replaced the traditional system. Steady progress was made in developing secular public education[24] as a tool to convert the Tibetan people to communism.

With reforms in agriculture, advances in industrial development, road construction, domination of commerce, and effective political and administrative control, the Chinese succeeded in creating in Tibet in the early 1960s an economic and political system subservient to Peking. The abolition in 1961 of the Panchen Lama's Council marked the end of the last traditional political institution in Shigatse.[25] Under the titular leadership of the Panchen Lama, the Chinese then completed arrangements for elections to establish people's councils at *hsien* and *hsiang* (village) levels in the various administrative regions.[26]

In 1965, after China's full political, administrative, and economic hold was secured, the official designation "autonomous region" was conferred on Tibet.[27] Nagbo Nawang Jigme, a Tibetan nobleman who had been the leading collaborator with the Chinese since the 1950s, was named to head the new government on September 9, 1965. His task (under the authority of General Chang Kuo-hua) was to guide Tibet's integration with China. The outbreak of the Cultural Revolution in 1966, however, pushed the new government into obscurity before it could serve its intended purposes.

1966–1968: *The Cultural Revolution*

During China's Great Proletarian Cultural Revolution, a movement set in motion by Chairman Mao Tse-tung to purge the Chinese Communist Party and government bureaucracy, the Red Guards—young militants—poured into Tibet, as well as other parts of China, to overthrow "capitalist power holders" among the Communist Party and government officials. Between August 1966 and August 1968 the Cultural Revolution in Tibet was marked by extensive housecleaning of the local administration, dismissal of a large number of trained Tibetan cadres, and elimination of the "four olds"—old culture, old customs, old habits, and old thoughts. During this period as thousands of young Red Guards smashed the party and the bureaucracy, Tibet replicated the confusion that characterized most of China. For a brief time, the upheaval resulting from the activities of the Red Guards and the struggle for supremacy among the revolutionary factions loosened the Chinese grip on the country and encouraged Tibetan resistance.

General Chang Kuo-hua, commander of the 1950 invasion forces and the dominant military and political figure on the plateau, was apprehensive of disorder and division among the Chinese in a country with a rebellious native population, and was determined to minimize the impact of the Cultural Revolution in Tibet. Despite his efforts, however, the Red Guards created widespread confusion in Lhasa and outlying towns. On August 25, 1966, they sacked the Jokhang, the main temple of Lhasa. Religious texts and

Kong), no. 584 (July 15, 1959): 11-15; "Final Report on 2nd Plenary Session of Preparatory Committee for Tibet Autonomous Region," *Current Background*, no. 586 (August 6, 1959); *New York Times*, July 4, 1959, p. 1.

[24] *Survey of China Mainland Press*, no. 2074 (August 12, 1959): 34; no. 2136 (November 19, 1959): 26; no. 2186 (February 1, 1960): 35.

[25] Ibid., no. 2495 (May 12, 1961): 26.

[26] Ibid., no. 2489 (May 4, 1961): 21; no. 2811 (September 4, 1962): 24.

[27] Derek J. Waller, *The Government and Politics of Communist China* (New York: Doubleday, 1971), p. 143.

paintings were set afire; images were destroyed and dumped into the river. All articles connected with the traditional ways of life were seized from private homes and destroyed. There were similar activities in Shigatse and other places.

An essential conflict of attitude existed between the representatives of the Cultural Revolution and the regular administrative authorities. General Chang, responsible for the maintenance of law and order, considered the Red Guard activities dangerous and provocative. The latter, to destroy the "counter-revolutionary line of the bourgeoisie," attacked and seized government buildings and succeeded in taking over organs of power from regular authorities. In 1966 a command of the Revolutionary Rebels of the People's Committee temporarily replaced the administration of General Chang, who was accused by the Red Guards of dereliction of duty, of "following the capitalist road," and of "empire building" in Tibet.[28] But units of the People's Liberation Army under Chang moved against the Red Guards, arrested key leaders, and regained control of the situation by the middle of March 1967. A major consequence of this event was complete militarization of the administration of Tibet.

Shortly after this, General Chang was transferred to Szechwan and Tseng Yung-ya was appointed commander of the Tibetan Military Region. In September 1968, he was also named chairman of the Revolutionary Committee formed during the Cultural Revolution to replace the old governing body. The Revolutionary Committee became the effective governing apparatus in Tibet, as in most of China's administrative units, institutionalizing the Cultural Revolution. Although the Committee represented a political compromise in that it included representatives of the various Chinese factions in Tibet, the army continued to maintain a dominant role and wield decisive power.

1969–1974: Tibet Today

The period immediately following the Cultural Revolution was characterized by major socialist transformation of the economy, outbreaks of insurgency among the population and consequent intensification of repression by the Chinese, a power struggle between contending factions among the Han settlers, and a growing Chinese military build-up on the plateau.

Both agriculture and stockbreeding were in the process of profound change. Agricultural collectivization was accelerated and by 1971, nearly 666 communes were operating in 34 percent of the *hsiang*.[29] In establishing communes, the Chinese confiscated property belonging to Tibetans. A drive to increase productivity and curtail consumption reduced the Tibetans to the status of laborers subordinate to the Han commune workers. Despite energetic pushing, nevertheless, the work of organizing communes moved slowly because of strong Tibetan resistance. According to refugees who fled the country in 1970, collectivization had produced food shortages in various parts of Tibet.[30]

Major changes were reported also in industry and transportation. Coal mines, chemical plants, and building material and machinery plants were established at several places. A large number of small or medium-sized hydroelectric power stations went into operation in 1971. The highway network continued to expand so that more than 90 percent of the *hsien* in Tibet now have motor vehicle transport.

China's claims of prosperity, economic development, and overwhelming admiration for Chairman Mao among the inhabitants of the plateau contrast with the views of Tibetan refugees and news reports in the world press. The guerrilla warfare in Tibet continues sporadically and recently departed (1972) refugees report discontent.[31] There are

[28] "Power Struggles in Tibet Region Described," *Communist China Digest* (Washington, D.C.: U. S. Department of Commerce, Joint Publications Research Service), no. 196 (March 18, 1968): 109-13.

[29] "People's Communes in Tibet," *China Pictorial* (Peking), no. 6 (1971): 20.

[30] For refugee accounts, see Peter Hazelhurst, "Tibet: The Silent War against the Chinese," *Times* (London), December 28, 1970, p. 8.

[31] Personal communications to the author from refugees in Nepal, Sikkim, and Bhutan. For reports of executions in Lhasa, Shigatse,

stories of Tibetans being rounded up, questioned, made to sign confessions, and hauled up before "people's courts" for alleged counterrevolutionary activities. The mass arrests and executions provide a clear indication that China has been encountering a fresh wave of discontent and opposition,[32] particularly since the introduction of communes.

Ever since the Cultural Revolution, which divided the Chinese themselves, the problems of factionalism and bourgeois anarchism at all levels have persisted in Tibet, and the dual questions of disunity and minority separatism have continued to present difficult problems for the Chinese. With the loss of Tibetan leaders such as the Dalai Lama and later the Panchen Lama, who served as figureheads the Chinese have encountered major problems in governing Tibet. In 1964 the Panchen Lama, who is reported to have become increasingly alienated by Peking's Tibetan policies, was publicly denounced as a reactionary by Chou En-lai and was removed from office in 1965 when he refused to cooperate with the Chinese. Refugee sources report that he disappeared from public life in 1969 and is believed to have died in prison.[33]

Large numbers of primary and secondary schools have been established in the past four years to ensure continuation of the political indoctrination of young people and to meet the needs of socialist revolution and construction. With Chinese culture taught in Tibetan schools and the People's Liberation Army commanders in key administrative roles, the Chinese are attempting to root out Tibetan culture. Each element of Tibetan self-identity—religion, customs, and culture—contains some seeds of anti-Han feeling, and until the Chinese succeed in exterminating the Tibetan culture, it will pose a political threat. Therefore, the onslaught of Chinese culture and Mao's ideology continues. By 1971 it was reported that a large number of Tibetans had participated in Mao Thought Study classes[34] and that some liberated serfs could repeat as many as a hundred of Mao's quotations from memory. The Soviet-sponsored Radio Peace and Progress has accused the Chinese of spreading Han culture in the educational system, of changing minority songs, languages, and holidays, and of forcing intermarriage to eliminate the Tibetan culture, in contrast to Soviet Central Asia, where it claims that regional culture and religion have been preserved.[35]

From the outset, China was developing Tibet as a major military bastion from which to project its power and influence into the border region with India. It also affords an important adjunct to Chinese defense against the Soviet Union in Sinkiang. Although the occupation has always been plagued by serious logistical problems necessitating an intensive effort to improve the communications network, including truck roads, construction of air bases, and development of an air supply system, China has maintained a garrison of perhaps as many as 250,000 to 300,000 troops in Tibet. This force level is considered sufficient to cope with internal security problems and the "pacification" of Tibet, and to deal with the possibility of hostilities against India.

During the last few years construction of airfields, supply depots, storage bunkers, huge arsenals, and a massive system of tunnels and trenches camouflaged against aerial reconnaissance has been reported. All these provide evidence of considerable military build-up. Since 1970, there have also been indications of actual warlike preparations in Tibet. Important strategic installations connected with the Chinese nuclear program have been transplanted from areas in Sinkiang to safer and less accessible regions in Tibet. As a part of these "war preparations" the People's Liberation Army has mobilized almost the entire population, male and female, for tasks in support of the troops.

Tibet today is a land which is being pushed into the modern world at a great cost to its people and culture.

Gartok, and Yatung, see Tibetan News Agency releases, June 3, 1970; August 6, 1970; October 6, 1971.

[32] *New York Times*, September 5, 1971, p. 8.

[33] See the speech of General Chang Kuo-hua on September 2, 1965, reported in *Peking Review* 8, no. 39 (September 24, 1965): 20-22. See also *New York Times*, September 12, 1969, p. 10.

[34] *Great Changes in Tibet* (Peking, 1972), p. 38.

[35] See for example Hedrick Smith, "Islam Retaining a Strong Grip on Uzbeks," *New York Times*, November 22, 1972, p. 8.

There have been major achievements in health and in social and economic development, but these have come at a high price. China has pushed a vigorous policy of assimilation and integration of Tibet into the Han culture, where Tibetans might well have preferred benign neglect. Tibetans and other national minorities in China have never been considered equal to the Hans and since the Cultural Revolution Tibetans have come to occupy an even lower status in their own country. In 1973 it was reported that the Chinese were willing to have the Dalai Lama back in Tibet as head of the church but not as a secular head,[36] and the Dalai Lama had offered to go back to Lhasa on the condition that the Chinese hold an internationally super-vised plebiscite on the future of Tibet. The politically conscious young Tibetan leaders in India are in favor of rapprochement with China if China can give assurance of free elections within a year of the Dalai Lama's return and the appointment of Tibetan officials to positions now held by Chinese. A Tibetan government headed by the Dalai Lama and responsible for all internal affairs seems unlikely, and the terms of the Dalai Lama's return to Lhasa, if it happens, will be a matter of hard bargaining between the Tibetan leaders and the Chinese.

[36] "The Chinese May Be Loosening Their Grip on Tibet," *Economist* 249 (October 6, 1973): 37-38; ibid., 249 (November 3, 1973): 8.

4

THE COLONIALIZATION OF
TIBETAN POLITICS

BEFORE the Chinese invasion the political administration of Tibet was based on landed property, and ownership of land determined the role one was expected to play in the government of the country. Since noblemen and monasteries owned most of the land, the sons of noblemen and monks from wealthy monasteries were responsible for public service and civil administration. In essence the aristocracy together with the monks governed Tibet.

At the top of the political hierarchy was the Dalai Lama, who combined both spiritual and political power. As the earthly presence of Chenrezi, the patron god of Tibet, the powers of the Dalai Lama were in theory absolute.[1] In practice the Dalai's power was limited by authorities surrounding him, particularly the senior monks. Only outstanding individuals, such as the Fifth and Thirteenth Dalai Lamas, were successful in exercising full control of state affairs. A Council of Ministers (*kashag*), composed of three laymen and one monk all nominated by the Dalai Lama, assisted him.[2] The Council made decisions on all administrative, judicial, and political matters. Although each Council member was responsible for a particular area of government, Council decisions were made collectively. The Council appointed ecclesiastical officials and civil servants and received petitions against decisions taken by provincial governors, particularly those relating to disputes between influential families. Council decisions could be appealed to the Dalai Lama,

whose decision was supreme. At irregular intervals a Tibetan General Assembly,[3] made up of religious dignitaries, civil servants, aristocrats, and representatives of merchants and artisans, met and reached decisions by a majority vote.

Administratively various historical-political provinces of Tibet such as Kham, Tsang, and Ngaris were subdivided into districts or *dzongs*. The important districts were administered by two officials, a layman from a noble family and a monk, who often assisted each other. Among other things, district governors were responsible for collecting taxes and administering justice.[4] Governors farther away from Lhasa were less subject to the control of the central government. Generally the district governors far from Lhasa, especially those along the frontiers with control over trade routes, abused their power to secure financial advantages.

[1] For the doctrine of government in traditional Tibet as viewed against the ideological background of Lamaism, see Nirmal Chandra Sinha, *Prolegomena to Lamaist Polity* (Calcutta: F. K. L. Mukhopadhyay, 1969).

[2] Between 1926 and 1940 an office of prime minister (Silon) existed in Tibet. The post was abolished in 1940 but was reestablished in 1950 by the Fourteenth Dalai Lama, who appointed a lay administrator and a high monk to hold the office jointly. At the insistence of the Chinese they were removed from office in late 1951, and the post of prime minister was liquidated.

[3] See Thubten Jigme Norbu and Colin M. Turnbull, *Tibet* (New York: Simon and Schuster, 1968), pp. 325-28.

[4] H. E. Richardson, *A Short History of Tibet* (New York: Dutton, 1962), p. 22.

For defense the Tibetan government maintained an army of 10,000 men, whose main task was to parade on the Tibetan New Year festival. The majority of the poorly trained and ill-equipped militia were supplied by landowners. The military administration was headed by two officials, an ecclesiastic and a layman.[5]

Changes in Political Organization

In their initial attempt to assert control over Tibet, the Chinese recognized three regional administrations based at Lhasa, Shigatse, and Chamdo. They used the Panchen Lama, based at Shigatse, and Nagbo Nawang Jigme, governor of the Chamdo territory, to reduce the authority of the central government at Lhasa. Until 1964, the Panchen Lama spoke unhesitatingly with Peking's voice, assuring Tibetans that their future lay in a new Tibet of Chinese design. While a Chinese-appointed committee administered Tibet, the Panchen served as the vice-chairman of the Preparatory Committee for the Autonomous Region of Tibet set up in 1955. Until his flight to India in 1959 the Dalai Lama served as chairman.

The Preparatory Committee was set up five years after the first Chinese soldiers marched into Tibet and four years after a seventeen-point agreement was reached in which China promised not to interfere in the internal administration and religious affairs of Tibet. Nevertheless, the work of the committee was hampered by rebellion in various parts of Tibet resulting from increasing erosion of the political and religious rights of the people. The Dalai Lama and the Tibetan masses had made it clear to the Chinese that whatever changes there were to be, they would accept them only under Tibetan management. Faced with this obstacle, China planned to continue the "local government" under the Dalai Lama until more members of the Tibetan upper strata were won over to the Chinese side. After the 1959 uprising, however, the Chinese decided to change the administrative structure.

An electoral law was published in 1961. Elections for various local bodies (people's councils at the *hsien* level) began in 1962 and went on steadily until 1964. Progressive and liberated serfs were encouraged to stand as candidates for these elections.[6] In September 1965, the Tibetan Autonomous Region was formally established with Nagbo as head of the new government, although General Chang Kuo-hua, commander of the invasion forces, remained the dominant political and military authority until 1967.

As mentioned earlier, the Chinese in 1966 divided Tibet into six political units which were further subdivided into seventy *hsien*, or counties. Each *hsien* was divided into communes, and each commune was politically and economically divided into production brigades and production teams organized by the people's councils. Most of the sub-*hsien* administrative units had neither geographical nor historical sanction. Local government on all levels was dominated by the Chinese army. The central government was essentially the administrative mechanism through which the top military leader, General Chang, who was also First Secretary of the Tibetan Communist Party, ruled the country. Political power was concentrated by a continuing process of assimilation into the party of all elite groups that occupied strategic positions.

Mao Tse-tung's Cultural Revolution involving "purge and power struggle" reached Tibet in May 1966 with the arrival of 500 Red Guards in Lhasa. Serious disturbances afflicted Tibet throughout the next two years and factionalism followed the seizure of power by Maoist elements.[7]

In late 1967, General Chang was promoted and moved to Szechwan as First Secretary of the Communist Party Provincial Committee.[8] The few high Tibetan officials were

[5] For the organization of Tibet's army see Lowell Thomas, Jr., *The Silent War in Tibet* (New York: Doubleday, 1959), pp. 81-83.

[6] Details of these elections, such as the number of Tibetan candidates, the number of Tibetans voting, and the results of the voting, are not available. Radio Lhasa reported that local elections were completed in most areas of Tibet in early 1963. See *Survey of China Mainland Press* (American Consulate General, Hong Kong), no. 2811 (September 4, 1962): 24.

[7] See chapter 3 above for details.

[8] Chang's promotion despite his opposition to Red Guard activity

removed or demoted by the Red Guards, and Chang was replaced by Tseng Yung-ya, a leftist.

The factionalism accompanying the Cultural Revolution in Tibet has continued to be strong down to the present. At least 700 people, including 250 Tibetans, were killed in February-March 1968 in skirmishes between rival groups in Lhasa and Shigatse.[9] Again in January, May, and August 1969, several people were killed or injured in Lhasa in fighting between two rival groups of Mao supporters, the Great Alliance and the Revolutionary Rebel Headquarters, both drawn from Chinese colonists. The August 1969 incident involved not only the rival factions but also the Lhasa garrison. The trouble occurred after a meeting at which both factions were ordered by the army to hand in their arms and ammunitions, and both rejected the order. Chinese troops in Tibet were instructed to remain neutral during the factional fighting, but armories were looted by insurgent groups. The civil war among the pro-Mao and anti-Mao forces offered the Tibetan resistance fighters new opportunities in the guerrilla war they had been waging since 1951. Armed with Russian rifles and ammunition captured from the Chinese, resistance fighters generally operate in local pockets. One of these is reportedly based on Nepal's border, and has occasionally received arms drops from unmarked aircraft.[10] During 1970 there were reports of violent clashes between the Tibetan rebels and the Chinese, as well as between the rival Chinese factions and army units, each trying to obtain a share of political power.

In September 1968 the Revolutionary Committee was established as the new governing body of Tibet, with Tseng Yung-ya as chairman. Revolutionary committees at provincial, subprovincial, and *hsien* levels replaced the people's councils and other existing governmental bodies. The establishment of these revolutionary committees completed the "seizure of power" phase of Mao's Cultural Revolution throughout China, including the autonomous regions of Tibet and Sinkiang. Consolidation of the functions of the army-dominated revolutionary committees at various levels is currently tightening China's control over Tibet.

In 1969 the Tibet Revolutionary Committee urged the rival factions to make peace and support the army. Yet despite repeated appeals for unity and the personal intervention of Mao Tse-tung, factionalism and anarchism continue to trouble Tibet. In 1969 China acknowledged the need for a more experienced official in Tibet by appointing Tien Pao, a veteran official of Tibetan origin, as vice-chairman of the Revolutionary Committee. The Committee eliminated the earlier policy of relaxed rule in outlying areas by extending the harsh rule which had previously prevailed only in central Tibet.

Tibet's Communist Party Committee, formed in August 1971, is dominated by military men and by individuals who are categorized as moderates or pragmatists. The new party chief is Jen Jung, who replaced Tseng Yung-ya as acting chairman of the Revolutionary Committee in June 1971. Tseng disappeared from the public scene. Three of the six secretaries under Jen are military men and like Jen are Han Chinese. The three civilian secretaries are Tibetan.[11]

The Chinese have managed to create a new Tibet with a thriving political and economic structure having recognizable coherence and personality, distinct from the pre-1951 Tibet. But the special identity of today's Tibet was brought from China proper by the Han people. Han authority and communist ideology affect so many phases of Tibet's geography so deeply that one can interpret the spatial organization of the country today only by reference to the goals of both these forces.

The Political Future of Tibet

More than twenty years after the Chinese Army marched into Lhasa, Tibet remains one of the most troubled regions

---

indicates the enhanced position of the functionaries who run remote regions of China.

[9] *Times* (London), March 12, 1968, p. 1; Richard Harris, "Chinese against Chinese in Tibet Strife," ibid., December 4, 1968, p. 6.

[10] *Times* (London), February 17, 1967, p. 1.

[11] *New York Times*, September 5, 1971, p. 8; August 26, 1971, p. 5; "New Party Committees Established," *Peking Review* 14, no. 36 (September 3, 1971): 7.

under China's occupation. In establishing political control, China has had to cope with a sensitive border, a rebellious population, and contending factions among the Chinese sent to settle there. Military preponderance and communications supremacy have made it possible for China to maintain its domination and to augment its determination to assimilate Tibet into the Chinese nation. Although referred to as an autonomous region, Tibet, like other non-Han areas, is ruled under the direction of the Chinese central government. The Chinese have been successful in liquidating all the vestiges of Tibet's age-old theocratic government. Barring unexpected developments, it seems clear that total assimilation with China and consequent annihilation of the distinctive character of Tibet lie ahead.

The Dalai Lama, as sovereign head of the Tibetan government in exile, promulgated a new constitution for Tibet in 1963. The Dalai hopes that Tibet will some day again be an independent nation. The new constitution takes into consideration the doctrines enunciated by Buddha, the temporal and spiritual heritage of Tibet, and the ideas and ideals of the modern world. On the tenth anniversary of the Tibetan uprising, in March 1969, the Dalai Lama said, "When the day comes for Tibet to be governed by its own people, it will be for the people to decide as to what form of Government they will have. The system of governance by the line of the Dalai Lamas may or may not be there. It is the will of the people that will ultimately determine the future of Tibet."[12] The world community has continued to ignore the Dalai Lama's claim of independence for Tibet and his 1950 appeal to the United Nations for help. His further appeals in 1959, 1961, and 1965 have brought forth only U.N. resolutions calling for respect of human rights in Tibet.[13]

World opinion has taken little notice of the plight of Tibet. In 1959 the Soviet Union asserted that Tibet was an internal matter for China and described the Tibetan revolt as an affair of reactionaries supported by "imperialist circles and Chiang Kai-shekites." The Soviet attitude toward Tibet changed in 1967 with the growing border dispute and the intensifying ideological wrangle between China and the USSR.[14] The few Tibetan "reactionaries" of 1959 in Soviet reports suddenly turned, in 1967, into tens of thousands of Tibetans fighting for national freedom.

Soviet support of the Tibetan freedom fighters has aroused new hope among some Tibetan exiles. They derive solace from the reported asylum granted to some of the associates of the Panchen Lama in Mongolia and Siberia. The signing in 1971 of a twenty-year treaty of peace and cooperation between India and the Soviet Union—two of China's principal adversaries—has given China new cause for concern about security in Tibet and Sinkiang. India and Russia have become invaluable to one another in that they can exert pressure on China's borders from different points of the compass. With the dismemberment of Pakistan and the creation of Bangladesh, India emerged in 1972 as the dominant power south of Tibet. The destruction of the old balance of power between India and Pakistan removed the only rival to Indian supremacy along the southern fringes of China from Iran to Indochina. The dogged Soviet support for the establishment of Bangladesh succeeded in humiliating the Chinese by creating a friendly state along the southern rim of Asia.

The Dalai Lama, deeply imbued with the Buddhist spirit of love, toleration, and forgiveness, shows no rancor or hatred for the Communist Chinese. In his statement of March 10, 1960, he called upon his countrymen to dedicate themselves to the "achievement of a free Tibet governed by Tibetans themselves." He reminded the Chinese "that oppression [has] never, anywhere, succeeded in suppressing the eternal desire of people to live as free men." What

[12] "Statement of His Holiness the Dalai Lama on the Occasion of the Tenth Anniversary of the Tibetan National Uprising," *Tibetan Review* (Darjeeling) 2, no. 3 (March 1969): 22-23.

[13] United Nations Documents A/4234, A/4848.

[14] Harrison E. Salisbury, "Soviet Chinese Hostility Found along the Frontier," *New York Times*, August 17, 1966; William Beecher, "Russians and Chinese Continue Wide Military Build-up along Disputed Border," ibid., July 22, 1970, p. 5; P. P. Karan, "The Sino-Soviet Border Dispute," *Journal of Geography* 63 (1964): 216-22.

sustains the Dalai and his people is the spirit of Buddha, who said, "However strong the storm of evil or untruth may be, it cannot totally extinguish the lamp of truth." In India now the Dalai Lama succors thousands of his countrymen who have followed him into exile. There he constantly works to bring the plight of Tibet before the eyes and conscience of the world. In March 1970 he said, "Many of the Tibetans may be ideologically communist but they are definitely nationalist communist. To these Tibetans, their nation comes first, ideology second. We are fighting against colonialism and not against communism."[15] In March 1974 he reiterated this position, saying, "According to the Mahayana School of Buddhism you sacrifice for the benefit of others, for the good of suffering humanity. So is the goal of communism. . . . We are not against communism. The struggle is really against Chinese domination and it will continue till the good day comes and the Chinese leave Tibet."[16]

[15] *Asian Recorder* 16, no. 17 (April 23-29, 1970): 9502-03.
[16] "Diplomacy and the Dalai Lama," *Far Eastern Economic Review* 83, no. 11 (March 18, 1974): 22.

THE TRANSFORMATION OF
THE TIBETAN ECONOMY

THE traditional economic system of Tibet was conditioned by religious attitudes. The conspicuous landscape features associated with economic activities up to 1951 can only be understood by reference to religion. Likewise the economic transformation since 1951 must be assessed in terms of the intense impress of communist ideology.[1] By replacing the old economic structure, in which monasteries and feudal estates controlled the use and development of natural resources, wealth, and trade, with government ownership and operation of industrial, commercial, and transport facilities, collectivization of agriculture, and emphasis on military industries, China has successfully impregnated the Tibetan landscape with the marks of communist economic theory.

The Economic Situation before 1951

Before the Chinese occupation, the spatial economic organization of Tibet was made up of two major sectors. The first was large estates, owned by the monasteries, the government, and the nobility, who exercised extensive rights and special privileges over the inhabitants in their areas in matters such as collection of taxes, justice, and administration. The monks and nobles formed closely connected politico-economic groups. The second sector was the peasant holdings in which land was granted to the peasant household directly by the state for production and manage-

ment and the peasant was obligated to pay taxes and services directly to the state. Economic affairs were viewed in both sectors first and foremost in light of their bearing on the well-being of religion.[2]

Although sparse data do not permit full delimitation of regional differences in the land system, it appears that the large estates formed the dominant unit of economic production and the basic type of land pattern in the densely settled areas of central and southern Tibet, whereas peasant holdings were predominant in western Tibet. With 43 percent of the land held by the monasteries, as compared with 35 percent by the government and 22 percent by the nobility in central and southern Tibet, the monasteries dominated the Tibetan economy.[3] Monastic estates, granted free of dues by the ruler, comprised holdings given either to a central monastery or to one of its subdivisions, such as a "college" within the monastery or even a small group

[1] See E. A. J. Johnson, *The Organization of Space in Developing Countries* (Cambridge, Mass.: Harvard University Press, 1970), pp. 1-27; S. Rohio, "Ideology and Rural Development," *East Africa Journal*, May 1972, pp. 29-31.

[2] For an excellent summary of the pre-1951 economic structure see Pedro Carrasco, *Land and Polity in Tibet* (Seattle: University of Washington Press, 1959); see also Melvyn C. Goldstein, "Taxation and Structure of a Tibetan Village," *Central Asiatic Journal* 15, no. 1 (1971): 1-27.

[3] Charles Bell, *The Portrait of the Dalai Lama* (London: Collins, 1946), p. 165.

of monks belonging to the particular monastery. Income from the religious estates was used for the support of the cult.

The estates of the nobility were granted to noble families by the state. The holders of these land grants performed service for the government and exercised the state's right of taxation and justice over the inhabitants. Peasants living on the estate had to provide all labor needed for farming the land, maintaining the landlord's household, weaving cloth and rugs, and providing transportation for the landlord. The agriculturally productive and heavily populated areas in central Tibet, particularly around Lhasa, Gyantse, and Shigatse, contained a large concentration of estates owned by nobility and monasteries.

The landholdings assigned to various offices and to the army comprised government or treasury estates. These lands yielded income to various treasuries, such as the principal government treasury, the Dalai Lama's private treasury, or the army treasury. Land on these estates was cultivated by peasants of the district who paid taxes to the district official. The income from the estates along with a portion of funds allocated from the government's general revenue met the needs of the various offices. The two district governors (one a monk, the other a lay official) in each of Tibet's districts were responsible for the management and collection of revenues from government estates.[4]

Land held from the state and cultivated by a single peasant family paying taxes and services directly to the state formed the peasant holdings in pre-1951 Tibet. The distribution of peasant holdings is difficult to discuss in detail because precise information is unavailable, but it appears that peasant holdings were relatively dominant in the Chumbi Valley and the western part of the plateau. The regular peasant landholders sometimes rented their land to landless peasants.

The estates of monasteries and noblemen not only occupied the fertile agricultural valleys but extended into pasture lands on the adjacent mountain slopes. With the exception of a small number of nomads (horpa) who owned

animals themselves, the vast majority of herdsmen grazed cattle, sheep, goats, and yaks belonging to the nobles or monasteries. Each year at a specified month, shepherds were obliged to deliver the agreed proportion of animals to their owners.

The unduly dominant economic position of the landed gentry and ecclesiastical hierarchs created a wide disparity between the levels of living of the nobility and wealthy monks on the one hand and the peasantry and shepherds on the other. The landed aristocracy and monasteries were committed to perpetuation of the traditional economic system and both were in general opposed to reforms and modernization which would endanger their entrenched economic position. China's attempt to use economic reforms, particularly changes in land tenure, to undermine the power of the nobility and monasteries and to curry favor among the peasantry and herdsmen did bring some positive response from the lower classes between 1951 and 1959. After the 1959 uprising the sweeping "land reform" program resulted in complete elimination of the old landed interests which had been the focal point of opposition to Chinese Communist policies. Between 1951 and 1959, and particularly in 1959–1960, groups of Tibetans led by Han cadres denounced monks and members of the nobility who held most of the land, condemning many to death or imprisonment.

The Reorganization of Agriculture

During the last twenty years, far-reaching changes have occurred in Tibetan agriculture, the most important occupation on the plateau. These changes have not only profoundly altered the farming patterns and practices but have also revolutionized the agricultural system by dramatic expropriation and redistribution of agricultural land. In 1951 Tibet was largely a country of huge estates owned by nobility and monasteries. By 1970, 666 communes had

[4] David Macdonald, *The Land of the Lamas* (London: Seeley Service Co., 1929), pp. 57-58.

been established, covering one-third of the "townships" on the plateau.[5] The former owners of estates had lost their land, their superior status, their authority and prestige, and found themselves workers in communes engaged in collective production.

The first stage in this transformation involved seizure of lands from the nobility, monasteries, and wealthy families. Although some progress was made in the transference of land to tenant farmers and landless peasants before 1959, the first year following the uprising of 1959 saw the complete expunging of rich landowners. By April 1961, over 186,000 hectares had been distributed to 100,000 peasant households.[6] Similarly in pastoral areas animals once owned by nobility and raised by nomads were turned over to 4,800 poor shepherds.[7] The break-up of large estates and distribution of their land, draft animals, and implements to peasants and former serfs brought about a major change in the landscape of the plateau as small holdings appeared on the former estates.

The redistribution of land was quickly followed by systematic organization of groups of peasant households into mutual-aid teams—a major step in the direction of collective labor. The mutual-aid teams, which were later merged into agricultural producer's cooperatives, created favorable conditions for the setting up of collective farms and finally people's communes—the cherished goal of the communist regime. Eleven peasant households in Chiehpa, Naitung, were the first in Tibet to organize a mutual-aid team. Later this team merged into an agricultural producer's cooperative, and in 1966 it became part of a commune consisting of 200 households.[8] Over 90 percent of peasant households were organized into mutual-aid teams by November 1961. By the end of 1962 the mutual-aid teams had merged into 22,000 cooperatives embracing 166,000 households.[9] Members of the cooperative would pool their resources to meet the production targets set by the government.

In 1964 the first groups of agricultural cooperatives were merged to form an unspecified number of communes. One hundred and thirty more communes were set up at the end of 1965 and in early 1966. By the middle of 1970 a total of 666 communes had been established in Tibet.[10] By their large labor force, the communes are capable of reshaping the agricultural economy. In addition, the growth of communes in Tibet has facilitated vigilance and detection of sabotage activities, thereby strengthening the position of the Chinese in rural and pastoral areas. Communes along the Indo-Tibetan border have the added responsibility of cooperating with the People's Liberation Army frontier guards.

The communes have made impressive gains in the development of irrigation and effective use of water resources. This is particularly important in a country where intensive use of land is possible only through irrigation. In the agricultural valleys, irrigation is as old as farming, but was inefficient. Traditionally peasants provided the labor for the construction of irrigation works and the landowners cooperated in their upkeep. Small mountain streams were dammed to store water for agricultural purposes, but much valuable water was lost in flow. New methods have now been developed to prevent this water loss. As a result of the efforts of the communes, nearly 100,000 hectares of newly irrigated farmland had been developed in Tibet by 1966. The total irrigated area was reported to have grown 30 percent between 1959 and 1966. In 1971 more than 80 percent of Tibet's cultivated area was under irrigation.[11]

[5] *Peking Review* 13, no. 31 (July 31, 1970): 30; "People's Communes in Tibet," *China Pictorial*, no. 6 (1971): 18-21.

[6] *Survey of China Mainland Press* (American Consulate General, Hong Kong), no. 2471 (April 7, 1961): 18; no. 2635 (December 8, 1961): 29. For a good summary of change until 1960, and documentation, see George Ginsburgs and Michael Mathos, "Communist China's Impact on Tibet: The First Decade," *Far Eastern Survey*, July 1960, pp. 102-09; August 1960, pp. 120-24; *New York Times*, February 29, 1960, p. 8.

[7] *Survey of China Mainland Press*, no. 2635 (December 8, 1961): 29; *Times* (London), July 4, 1966, p. 8.

[8] "People's Communes in Tibet," *China Pictorial* (Peking), no. 6 (1971): 18.

[9] *Survey of China Mainland Press*, no. 2830 (October 2, 1962): 22.

[10] "Upsurge in Socialist Transformation of Agriculture and Livestock Breeding on Tibetan Plateau," *Peking Review* 13, no. 31 (July 31, 1970): 30.

[11] "Irrigation Projects Developed in Tibet and Sinkiang," *People's*

Water pumping stations were hoisting river water for irrigation of extensive areas. In order to provide irrigation for farmlands in the Shigatse area and to supply drinking water for the city of Shigatse, a canal was dug by the local commune.[12]

The commune of Liehmai in Lungtzu, formed in 1967, built two irrigation ditches totalling 30 kilometers on mountains more than 4,000 meters above sea level, displaying their mastery over nature. The melted snow flows through the ditches from the mountains to over 700 mu of newly reclaimed land sown to barley. The commune's output of grain in 1969 was almost three times that of 1959.[13] Similarly the 300 members of the Hsuchung commune successfully constructed a 280-meter-long tunnel during four years of work, redirecting the river water to irrigate more than 1,400 mu.[14] Similar achievements in irrigation and water management are reported from other communes.

Through the commune system, China has been able to make significant progress in introducing better agricultural methods, disseminating modern technical information, and exploiting virgin lands. Before 1951 land was plowed with wooden plows, there was little use of fertilizer, and the yield was low. In 1972 it was reported that "no trace is left of the primitive farm tools."[15] Tractor stations and farm implement factories on the plateau manufacture agricultural tools. Improved seeds, insecticides, chemical fertilizers, and vaccines for animals sent from China are transforming farming in Tibet.

Tibet's Institute of Agricultural Science and Shigatse Agricultural Experiment Farm have reportedly developed eight strains of wheat and five strains of barley which are resistant to drought and cold and are suitable for the plateau's climate and soil.[16] Production brigades and teams in many communes have their own experimental groups.

As a result of the development of irrigation, higher fertilizer application, improved mechanization, better seed selection, insect and disease control, and other techniques of intensive agriculture, the yield per area unit has made a substantial increase. The 1970 farm production in Tibet was more than double that of 1959,[17] and the 1970 grain production was 10 percent higher than that of 1969. The per-hectare yield outstripped the required targets in over fifty communes. In several communes the total output of grain in 1970 was reported almost three times the production in 1959.[18]

Double cropping (two harvests in one growing season) is reported along the Tsangpo River in southern Tibet. In the Phari area, adjoining Bhutan, the annual output of wheat and barley was reported to have trebled, from 100 tons in 1965 to 310 tons in 1966.[19]

In addition to improvement of existing farmland, which is concentrated in favorable areas below 12,000 feet in the Tsangpo Valley and on the terraces of its important tributaries, significant progress has been reported in the expansion of cultivated areas. Marginal lands amounting to 66,000 hectares were reportedly reclaimed for agricultural production during the past decade. It seems doubtful, however, that large-scale increases in agricultural area will be possible in the Chang Thang and mountainous areas of the north, which occupy nearly three-quarters of the country.

Among the cereal crops, barley is the most important, accounting for roughly one-third of all agricultural land, two-thirds of the area given to crops. The importance of

Daily (Peking), March 25, 1966; "Tibetan Peasants Tackle Irrigation Problem to Extend Farming Area Regularly Giving Good Harvests," New China News Agency, Lhasa, March 19, 1966. "Farming and Livestock Breeding Develop in Tibet," *Peking Review* 14, no. 31 (July 30, 1971): 13.

[12] "Changes in Tibet's Shigatse," *Peking Review* 15, no. 48 (December 1, 1972): 21.

[13] "Chairman Mao Guides Emancipated Serfs in Their Triumphant Advance," *Peking Review* 13, no. 41 (October 9, 1970): 34.

[14] *Peking Review* 14, no. 25 (June 18, 1971): 22.

[15] Hung Nung, "Farming and Stock Breeding Thrive in Tibet," *Great Changes in Tibet* (Peking: Foreign Languages Press, 1972), p. 50.

[16] "Agricultural and Livestock Scientific Research in Tibet," *Peking Review* 15, no. 3 (January 21, 1972): 4.

[17] Hung, "Farming and Stock Breeding," p. 49.

[18] "People's Communes in Tibet," *China Pictorial*, no. 6 (1971): 18.

[19] "Tibetan Farming Area High in the Himalayas Now Has Grain Surplus," New China News Agency, Lhasa, January 7, 1967; "Tibet Has Good Grain Harvest," ibid., September 19, 1966.

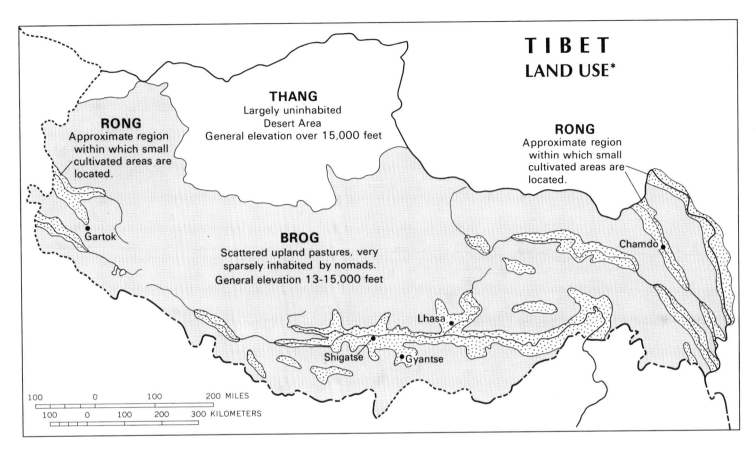

TIBET
LAND USE*

THANG
Largely uninhabited
Desert Area
General elevation over 15,000 feet

RONG
Approximate region
within which small
cultivated areas are
located.

RONG
Approximate region
within which small
cultivated areas are
located.

• Gartok

Chamdo •

BROG
Scattered upland pastures, very
sparsely inhabited by nomads.
General elevation 13-15,000 feet

Lhasa •

Shigatse • • Gyantse

100   0   100   200 MILES

100   0   100   200   300 KILOMETERS

barley reflects the steppe conditions. Recent estimates of its production and yield do not exist. However, it was reported early in this century that lands near Lhasa yielded six times the amount of seed sown in normal years.[20] In the past, cultivation and production suffered from heavy fluctuations in rainfall. The development of irrigation has reduced the impact of weather vagaries on crop production.

Wheat and buckwheat, grown mainly below 11,500 feet, are among the other extensively cultivated crops. In the past the area under wheat fluctuated from year to year, depending largely on weather conditions at the time of sowing, which comes in the autumn or in spring after the melting of snow. The development of high-yielding strains suitable for the climatic conditions on the plateau has increased the yield of this cereal.[21] The overall wheat yield before 1951 was low—estimated at about ten to twelve times the amount of seed sown.[22] In years of meager rain-

* Generalized pattern compiled from Survey of India map sheets (1921–1928) and updated by information from satellite photos.

[20] Ekai Kawaguchi, *Three Years in Tibet* (London: Theosophical Publishing Society, 1909), pp. 235-36.

[21] Hung, "Farming and Stock Breeding," p. 46; see also *Survey of China Mainland Press*, no. 2651 (January 4, 1962): 32; no. 2662 (January 19, 1962): 24.

[22] This estimate for central Tibet is based on information obtained

fall, with little snow on the ridges, very little water for irrigating wheat lands, and frequent drying winds, yields were markedly low. The highest yields came from irrigated, intensively cultivated lands, such as the Lhasa Plain. Mountain slopes with terraced fields have lower yields, with the highest terraces giving the lowest yields. Wheat is grown largely on rotation with barley. In some areas wheat is followed by peas. In the rich bottomlands of river valleys, from one-fifth to one-third of the land is given to wheat; on the slopes the percentage is lower.

Vegetables were grown in the past in the Lhasa Plain to supply the nobility and wealthy classes. Tibet is now growing as many as twenty-one different kinds of vegetables,[23] particularly tomatoes, cucumbers, and green peppers, in addition to radishes, potatoes, and turnips, grown before 1951. The area devoted to such fruits as apricots, peaches, pears, and walnuts, which occupied a small portion of the land in 1951, has been expanded. In pre-communist Tibet fruit orchards were largely the preserve of estate owners or other wealthy men, who enjoyed not only of the fruit but also the green aspect and cool shade. Communes in Naitung have recently established orchards with more than 20,000 apple trees.[24]

For the first time, tea, tobacco, and sugar beets are being successfully cultivated. A tea farm in Linchih processes its own tea leaves into black and green tea and tea bricks for local consumption, making it unnecessary to import tea from Szechwan and Yunnan.[25]

Improved breeds of cow introduced recently give twice as much milk as ordinary breeds in the past. Most communes have expanded the raising of hogs, which has increased the supply of fertilizer, thus augmenting the farm production as well as providing meat. The number of hogs in Tibet is now about four times that of 1959 and averages one per household in some communes.[26] A veterinarian service network provides animal disease prevention.

On the basis of meager official statistics, consisting only of scattered reports of percentage changes in crop yields and production, it is difficult to evaluate the growth of grain and other food production in Tibet. However, it appears that Tibetan farming has been modernized considerably and that there have been major improvements in agricultural practices.

Unfortunately little of the increased production seems to be reaching the Tibetans themselves. Refugees who escape report strict food rationing in both towns and rural areas. In some areas near-starvation conditions exist. Outside the official ration shops people queue endlessly for a few ounces of butter and coarse black bread. The average peasant is allowed fourteen kilos of barley or other food grain per month.[27] Chinese residents in Tibet are allowed higher food quotas, nearly seventeen kilos of rice or wheat a month. A Tibetan refugee in Sikkim, in a 1970 interview,[28] indicated that an adult's monthly ration of roasted barley was twenty-five pounds (about nine kilos) and that many Tibetans stood in queues all night in front of Chinese-run shops to make sure they got that much. Butter, cheese, milk, meat, and vegetables were reported scarce, with sugar available only on festive occasions.[29]

"At first we believed the Chinese when they said there would be prosperity for all," a Tibetan refugee reported during an interview in Pokhara, Nepal, in 1970. "They distributed land and for many of us it was the first land we had worked for ourselves. Then when our granaries began to fill they taxed and rationed us and nationalized all

from Tibetan farmers living in refugee camps in Sikkim. For other estimates of the yield of wheat and barley in various parts of Tibet before 1951, see Pedro Carrasco, *Land and Polity in Tibet* (Seattle: University of Washington Press, 1959), p. 9.

[23] *Peking Review* 14, no. 6 (February 5, 1971): 19.

[24] Ibid., 13, no. 31 (July 31, 1970): 31.

[25] Ibid., 15, no. 3 (January 21, 1972): 4.

[26] Hung, "Farming and Stock Breeding," p. 51; see also "Raising Pigs on Tibetan Plateau," *Peking Review* 14, no. 14 (April 2, 1971): 24.

[27] Peter Hazelhurst, "Tibet: The Silent War against the Chinese," *Times* (London), December 23, 1970, p. 8.

[28] From an extensive group of interviews I conducted in the Tibetan borderlands to gather materials on socioeconomic and political changes.

[29] A monthly ration of twenty-two to twenty-eight pounds of either barley or wheat flour, depending upon loyalty to the Chinese, was reported in *Times* (London), September 27, 1967, p. 1.

property. We own nothing now, not even our souls and our dignity." Despite official claims to the contrary severe drops in production followed the introduction of communes in Tibet, according to recent refugees.

Food shortages have not slackened Chinese ambitions in Tibet. As the number of Han settlers increases, Tibetan belts are tightened. In the words of a recently arrived refugee: "The Chinese are everywhere in Tibet, as thick as flies on a carcass."[30]

The Development of Pastoral Areas

In the extensive mountain pasture region, which the Tibetans refer to as *brog*, pastoral economy is dominant. Before 1951 about one-sixth of Tibet's population was estimated to be engaged in pastoralism.[31] Groups of herdsmen formerly grazed the livestock of monasteries and nobility in these areas, delivering an agreed proportion of animals to their feudal owners annually. During the winter the herders usually gathered in permanent settlements, then moved to grazing areas with the approach of summer. In all areas the migration of herds from valleys to high plateaus in summer and back in fall is common. In 1960 the livestock of estate owners were confiscated and turned over to the impoverished herdsmen who had tended them.[32]

On the bleak, desolate, arid high plains of northern Tibet known as *thang*, pastoral activities are limited to a few scattered areas of nomadic encampments. Here nomads living in tents move from pasture to pasture according to season with their herds of ponies, sheep, yak, and long-haired goats.

The quality of grass in the pastures of central Tibet is high, but the yield is generally low and varies a great deal. Some areas yield as much as fifteen quintals of dry hay per hectare, but others yield no more than one quintal.[33] Pastures used for grazing are mostly distributed in areas of high elevation. They are adequate for summer and autumn grazing but not for winter grazing because of the severe climate. Generally speaking, pastures located far from the populated areas are not fully used, while those in the vicinity of densely settled areas are overgrazed. The quality of grass in overgrazed areas degenerates with the emergence of weeds and cushioning plants.

The summer grazing pastures on the alpine slopes as well as the plateau grasslands are usable for three to four months of the year. They are suitable for yaks, sheep, and goats. Around the lake basins pastures may be used all year round. Winter pastures and fields in the lake marshes and around valleys provide taller grass which may be cut for hay.[34]

The Chinese have attempted to use the natural pastures of Tibet more effectively by regulating winter grazing of lower pasture lands, encouraging grazing of remote pasture areas in summer and fall, and delaying migration to winter and spring pastures. The productivity and utilization rate of pastures are being improved by rotated grazing.

Recent border controls have made unusable the mountain pastures adjoining the frontier areas of Tibet and neighboring India, Nepal, Sikkim, and Bhutan. In the past, herdsmen from Tibet and the adjoining Himalayan countries moved their sheep and goats into the high mountain pastures in summer, then retreated to lower altitudes in winter. Chinese frontier patrols have now ended this age-old pattern and animals on both sides of the frontier have suffered for lack of pasture. Herdsmen in Tibet have retreated northward toward the settled areas. In India, Nepal, and Sikkim some of the herdsmen must now earn a livelihood by working on border roads.

30 Interview with a Tibetan youth at Lachen, Sikkim, July 1970.

31 This is derived from the estimated five-sixths of the population stated to be engaged in agriculture, which leaves one-sixth or less engaged in pastoral activity. See R. A. Stein, *Tibetan Civilization* (Stanford: Stanford University Press, 1972), p. 109; Tsung-lien Shen and Shen-chi Liu, *Tibet and Tibetans* (Stanford: Stanford University Press, 1953), p. 130.

32 *Peking Review* 3, no. 13 (March 29, 1960): 17.

33 *Vegetation of Central Tibet* (Peking: Chinese Academy of Sciences, 1967), p. 83.

34 For an excellent discussion of nomadic pastoralism in northeast ethnic Tibet (outside the borders of political Tibet), see Robert B. Ekvall, *Fields on the Hoof: Nexus of Tibetan Nomadic Pastoralism* (New York: Holt, Rinehart and Winston, 1968).

In order to strengthen their control in pastoral areas, the Chinese initiated a policy of "fixed abode and nomadic herding." Beginning in 1958 "fixed residential points" were established for herdsmen,[35] from which they would lead animals to grazing grounds. Because the development of settled dwellings in pastoral areas involved changes in the herdsmen's habits of production and living, China encountered severe resistance initially. The plan to develop pastoral producers' cooperatives with fixed ranches and grazing grounds and access to pasture and water sources was delayed in 1959 because of opposition from herdsmen. By the early 1970s, however, many herdsmen had built houses and animal shelters and lived in permanent settlements.[36] A large number of Tibetan cadres, loyal to the proletarian revolutionary line, are working in the pastoral areas to bring about sedentarization of nomads. In Kuchang commune in Kaitse, western Tibet, more than a hundred mud-brick dwellings were built to settle the nomadic herdsmen, and similar reports have come from elsewhere on the plateau.[37]

Reorientation of Trade

For centuries, mountainous terrain and the dependence on tracks and pack animals for transport imposed on Tibet a pattern of local and regional isolation. At the opening of the twentieth century the British were able to establish commercial relations with Tibet, while a trade agency at Gyantse, according to the 1904 agreement, began to open Tibet to the modern world. Tibet's traditional trade with India, Nepal, Mongolia, and China moved over difficult paths and mule tracks, most of which were generally impassable during seasons of heavy snow. Yaks, the sturdy long-haired animals which can withstand the severe climate and travel ten to twelve hours a day with load, served as beasts of burden. Historically, the most important Tibetan trade route ran from Siliguri, an Indian railhead in north Bengal, to Kalimpong and across the frontier state of Sikkim to Gyantse and Yatung, the two leading trade marts in Tibet. Other principal trade routes into Tibet were from

Almora in the northern part of Uttar Pradesh, and from Simla over the India-Tibet road (a mere trail much of the way) to Gartok in western Tibet. From Almora to Gartok the route runs almost due north and from Simla to Gartok it is nearly due east. On the India-Tibet road, which follows the valley of the Sutlej River, there are no steep gradients. Yaks used for transport on this route carried about 240 pounds each and subsisted by grazing on the way. Nearly half of Tibet's trade with India was carried on the Siliguri-Kalimpong road, somewhat less than one-fourth passed through Almora and Simla, and the remainder through several other routes across the Himalayas. The central position of Gyantse at the junction of trade routes from India and Bhutan with those from Ladakh in Kashmir and from Central Asia, made it an important distributing center. Its location, 140 miles from Lhasa and 213 from Siliguri, offered it considerable advantage as a trade mart.

Profitable Indian commerce during the twentieth century resulted in the development of a wealthy Tibetan trading class in Lhasa and Shigatse,[38] the two principal commercial centers. Throughout this period the bulk of the Tibetan trade moved in and out on the Siliguri-Kalimpong-Lhasa route. Border towns in India such as Kalimpong, the largest entrepôt of Tibetan trade, and Almora, the next largest, remained major focal points for the Tibetan trade until the mid-1950s. In addition, Gartok acquired a share of the trade. In Tibet, imports arrived mostly in December, and the caravans left in March before the rivers were flooded. Tibet exported mainly wool to India and rock salt to Nepal, and imported a wide variety of merchandise from India, such as piece goods, rice, dyeing materials, ironware, sugar, tea, and

[35] *Survey of China Mainland Press*, no. 2375 (November 9, 1960): 27; Ekvall, *Fields on the Hoof*, pp. 96-97; Donald P. Whitaker and Rinn-Sup Shinn, *Area Handbook for the People's Republic of China* (Washington, D.C.: Government Printing Office, 1972), p. 292.
[36] "Farming and Livestock Breeding Develop in Tibet," *Peking Review* 14, no. 31 (July 30, 1971): 13-14.
[37] *China Pictorial*, no. 6 (1971): 27; *Great Changes in Tibet*, p. 29.
[38] David Snellgrove and H. E. Richardson, *A Cultural History of Tibet* (New York: Praeger, 1968), p. 235.

1960 the main items of Tibetan import included cotton textiles, sugar, tobacco, food, kerosene, gasoline, cement, steel, and finished wool products. Besides the customary items like yak tails and musk, raw wool, potatoes, and carpets accounted for most of the exports to India. During the eleven months beginning January 1959 the total value of goods imported from India was Rs. 6,040,000, compared with exports worth about Rs. 7,110,000. Both imports and exports during the first three months of 1959 were relatively high. But from April 1959, following the Tibetan uprising and the establishment of firm Chinese control over Tibetan trade, both imports and exports dwindled.[39] Now there is not even a smuggler's trail on the traditional trade routes across the Indo-Tibetan frontier which once bustled with activity during the trading season.[40]

Between 1911 and 1951, besides producing a wealthy Tibetan trading class, the traditional commerce between India and Tibet led many Tibetans to travel throughout India in quest of commercial products. An interest in the outside tobacco. Other interesting imports included mirrors, spectacles, umbrellas, soap, towels, and imitation gold foil. The Indian spectacles, largely of smoked or colored glass, were much desired by Tibetans because of the great glare of the sun and the dazzling reflections of the snow. The trade in Indian cotton piece goods included blue, printed, and fancy cloths. There was also considerable importation of Indian woolens and broadcloth. Chinese silk and damask for the robes of dignitaries and monks entered Tibet through the Siliguri-Kalimpong-Lhasa trade route rather than the difficult overland route from China to Lhasa.

In the 1950s Chinese supplies to Tibet began to flow through the port of Calcutta to Siliguri by rail and onwards to Kalimpong and Lhasa. This trade between India and Tibet, confirmed under the Sino-Indian Treaty of 1954, continued until the early 1960s. In January 1960 about 95 percent of the imports and exports were carried through Nathu La (pass) in Sikkim. The trade through Jelep La in Sikkim, which had amounted to one-fourth of the total trade, declined considerably between 1950 and 1960. In

world soon began to be felt among the traditionally isolated Tibetan elite.

Tibet's commerce with Nepal has existed on a small scale since ancient times. Until 1956, formal trade relations were based on the treaty of peace concluded in 1856, at the end of the second war between the two countries. The major commercial provisions of the treaty allowed Nepalese traders to reside and trade freely at Lhasa, and permitted the duty-free entry of Nepalese goods. The treaty also provided for the establishment of a Nepalese trading post at Lhasa, which was permitted to deal freely in all kinds of merchandise. Tibet also agreed not to levy taxes on goods imported by the Nepalese merchants nor to require them to pay any fees. A hundred years later, after successfully invading Tibet, the People's Republic of China signed a treaty with Nepal which permitted the nationals of both countries to trade with, travel in, and make pilgrimage to those places in each country as agreed upon by the two governments. Provision also was made for the establishment of an equal number of trade agencies of one government within the territory of the other at specified locations.[41] In addition to the agency at Lhasa, Nepal established trading posts at Kyirong, Kuti, and Shigatse. In 1961, China offered to construct a highway between Kathmandu and Lhasa, which would make possible an expansion of commercial relations.[42] An excellent all-weather highway from Kathmandu to the Tibetan frontier was completed in 1964. Despite this, Nepalese merchants are now being squeezed out of Tibet by the Chinese Trading Corporation and by the imposition of currency restrictions.

Tibet's trade with Bhutan flourished until 1953. It consisted of the import of woolen cloth, spices, rice, food grains,

[39] *Statesman* (Calcutta), January 19, 1960; *New York Times*, August 7, 1959, p. 1.
[40] For a discussion of the trans-Himalayan Indo-Tibetan trade see S. D. Pant, *The Social Economy of the Himalayas* (London: G. Allen and Unwin, 1935). For statistics on the volume of Indo-Tibetan trade in 1954 and 1956 see K. Beba, "Tibet Revisited," *China Reconstructs* (Peking), 6 (June 1957): 9-12.
[41] Eugene B. Mihaly, *Foreign Aid and Politics in Nepal: A Case Study* (New York: Oxford University Press, 1965), p. 57.
[42] Ibid., pp. 155-56.

handmade paper, and cheese from Bhutan and the export of wool, salt, and yak herds. Rice was particularly important, since it sold for Rs. 180 per maund (82 pounds) in Tibet as compared with Rs. 15 per maund in Bhutan. Because of Chinese aggressions and efforts to subject Bhutanese merchants to political indoctrination while in Tibet, the Bhutanese government decided to end this flourishing trade in 1959[43] and withdrew its trade representative from Lhasa in 1960.

The revival of Tibet's once flourishing trade with its southern neighbors appears unlikely. Indo-Tibetan trade has completely ceased. Traders from the Lahaul (Keylong) and Spiti (Kaza) areas in India who went to Tibet as late as 1959 reported harassment by the Chinese authorities, although the Tibetans themselves were cordial,[44] showed no reluctance to honor previous commitments and debts, and gave assurance that they would continue to honor them in future. Tibetans freely accepted Indian currency, though, as in previous years, they preferred food grains and tea, which fetched a higher price in terms of Tibetan goods— mostly wool and some salt. In 1960 prices were less steady than usual in a trade which had changed little for decades since it was largely governed by traditional agreements, or *phatties*, between corresponding valleys on both sides of the border. Volume of trade was also uneven in 1960, being less than usual at some trading marts and unexpectedly high at others.

Because of uncertainty, some Indian traders in 1959–1960 hung back well beyond the appointed dates by which, according to *phatties*, they were required to reach markets in Tibet. Some of their doubts stemmed from the arrival in Punjab and Himachal Pradesh of over 1,500 Tibetan refugees with their tales of disorder in Tibet, just before the start of the trading season. Even so, a surprising number of Indian traders began crossing the border, particularly at Doongbra, the appointed market for traders from the Baspa Valley (Kinnaur district, Himachal Pradesh). The Indian traders cited many specific examples of the willingness of the Tibetans to do business despite harassment from

the Chinese. The market at Doongbra, which is supposed to close down by a certain date each year after the middle of July, was kept open longer for the Indian traders who had been delayed by the border difficulties. And although this market is reserved, under its rules, for Baspa traders alone, eleven groups of Uttar Pradesh traders were also allowed to use it in 1959.

In early 1960 most traders in Lahaul, Spiti, and Chini were agreed that it would be best for the economy of border areas to normalize trade with Tibet if the Chinese authorities would be more consistent and cooperative. In 1960 most of the Tibetan traders were either held up at the border by the Chinese or allowed to come down only for a few days. In the Lahaul and Spiti region the bulk of the border trade used to be in the hands of petty traders. Finding an alternative means of livelihood for those who lived by commerce became imperative as a result of the complete cessation of trade between India and Tibet in 1961–1962.[45]

Until the 1951 Chinese occupation, the bulk of Tibet's trade with China was transacted at Kangting (formerly Tatsienlu) in Szechwan.[46] Its location, close to the geographical and ethnological boundary between China and Tibet, made it a convenient trade emporium. Most of the trade was transacted between the large Chinese firms in Kangting and the merchants who came in annually from Tibet. The majority of the Tibetan merchants brought with them native products to pay for the Chinese goods

[43] For details see Pradyumna P. Karan, *Bhutan: A Physical and Cultural Geography* (Lexington: University of Kentucky Press, 1967), p. 79.

[44] The materials in this section are based on my interviews with traders in Kalpa and Keylong in Himachal Pradesh.

[45] For recent economic changes in the Indian districts of Kinnaur, Lahul, and Spiti bordering Tibet, see Pran Chopra, *On an Indian Border* (New York: Asia Publishing House, 1964).

[46] Yak caravans took three and a half months to go from Lhasa to Tatsienlu by way of Batang. See Owen Lattimore, *Inner Asian Frontiers of China* (Boston: Beacon Press, 1962), p. 213. For a description of Tatsienlu see Peter Goullart, *Land of the Lamas* (New York: Dutton, 1959), pp. 12-21.

they bought. Some, however, were buyers only and brought gold dust or Chinese currency. Others were sellers only and took back with them Chinese silver currency. A few Tibetan merchants whose dealings were extensive were allowed from six to twelve months' credit and eventually settled their accounts with the Chinese firms by remitting the money to Shanghai via India.

The record of China's commercial policy during the first two decades of its rule in Tibet demonstrates its main concern to secure effective control over Tibet's trade and economy, to reorient Tibetan trade towards China, and to eliminate Tibet's traditional commercial links with India in particular and other countries in general. In the 1950s this new policy led to friction with merchants in both Tibet and India. Chinese commercial encroachments impinged on the interests of a large number of monks and noblemen. The policy of gradual diversion of Tibetan trade was abandoned after the uprising of 1959, when China assumed complete control. The diversion was facilitated by the development of highway transportation over the plateau. Increased amounts of Chinese goods, including daily necessities, medicines, tea, and manufactured articles, began to arrive in Tibet during the 1960s by way of newly built highways. The Chinese control altered not only the direction of trade but also its volume and composition.

The New Transportation Network

For centuries all transportation in Tibet was by porters and pack animals. In 1950 there was no other independent country of such a size in the world where no wheeled vehicles were used. Narrow, rough tracks linked the populated areas of the country, and principal rivers were unbridged. Yet most of the trails in southern and central Tibet were crowded with traffic during the summer and most commodities were transported along these trails by mule, sheep, or yak.

Chinese control brought a transformation to vehicular highways, built primarily with military and political goals rather than commercial intentions. The impact of the in- tensive development of modern transport and communications has been far-reaching, not only on the visible landscape but also on the implementation of communist social and economic programs. The new roads not only have altered the pattern of trade; they have also changed the general pattern of economic development of Tibet. The expansion of Tibet's road and air network has enabled China to move impressive numbers of Han personnel and large amounts of military equipment into areas hitherto accessible only by yak or foot, thereby increasing their political control and strengthening the military supply lines and relations with China proper.

Recognizing the importance of a transportation network in securing Tibet both politically and militarily,[47] China embarked upon a building program in 1952. Receiving top priority was the 1,000-mile Tsinghai–Lhasa railroad, which the Chinese hoped to complete in one year. The construction of this railroad was interrupted and postponed indefinitely, however, by the Khampa insurgency. A 300-mile military road in southwestern Tibet from Tingri airfield, north of Mount Everest, to Gartok, running parallel to the Nepalese border, was completed in 1960. Another 120-mile military road in southern Tibet linking Tse-tang with the border adjoining Towang in the North East Frontier Agency of India was completed in 1960.[48] A highway between Lhasa and Tse-tang had been completed earlier.

The network of new roads made it possible to stockpile huge amounts of military supplies at strategic points in Tibet, mostly fringing the southern borders. These supplies include gasoline, arms, food, and weapons,[49] all stored in giant artificial caverns. Hundreds of corrugated-roofed barracks of the People's Liberation Army have been constructed at various points along these new roads.

[47] *People's Republic of China: An Economic Assessment*, a compendium of papers submitted to the Joint Economic Committee, Congress of the United States (Washington, D.C., 1972), p. 162.

[48] *Statesman*, June 21, 1960. For the military purpose of these roads see Lowell Thomas, Jr., *The Silent War in Tibet* (New York: Doubleday, 1959), p. 207.

[49] *New York Times*, December 19, 1969, p. 6.

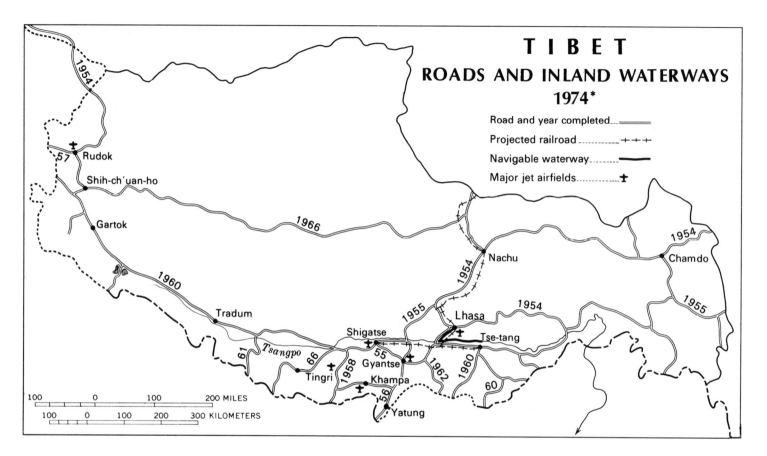

TIBET
ROADS AND INLAND WATERWAYS
1974*

Road and year completed............_____
Projected railroad.....................+ + +
Navigable waterway..............._____
Major jet airfields..................✈

By 1960 major progress had been made in linking Lhasa with China. A motorable road connecting Yaan in Szechwan with Lhasa by way of Chamdo was completed in late 1954.[50] The urban area of Chamdo is reported to have expanded six times since the completion of this highway.[51] Regular motor traffic began to operate in 1954 on the Tsinghai-Tibet road joining Sining (Hsi-ning) with Lhasa[52] and in 1955 this road was extended to Shigatse. A new motor road from Shigatse southeast to Gyantse was completed during the same year and was extended further south to Yatung in the Chumbi Valley in 1956. A number of feeder roads of widely varying types and degrees of service-ability were built to link the strategic areas in the south with the principal highways. By 1965, Tibet had an effective road network of 9,000 miles.[53] During 1967–1970 the Chinese extended roads and built outposts in the uninhabited mountain passes adjoining India for added security.

The road network completed and under construction in

* Based on official news releases and other published sources.
[50] New China News Agency, Lhasa, November 29, 1954.
[51] J. S. Prybyla, "Transportation in Communist China," *Land Economics* 42, no. 3 (1966): 274.
[52] Chang Po-chun, "First Highways to Tibet," *China Reconstructs* 4, no. 5 (May 1955): 2-5.
[53] *Times* (London), November 5, 1965, p. 10.

Tibet has been designed to meet the needs of the military. The needs of the Tibetan people or considerations of local economic development are secondary. By improving the highway network the Chinese have strengthened the ties of isolated nomadic elements with the Chinese-dominated centers and have made the task of controlling the plateau substantially easier. The roads were constructed by military personnel with the assistance of conscripted local workers and their maintenance is the responsibility of Han administrative and military personnel.[54]

The highways linking the three principal cities—Lhasa, Gyantse, and Shigatse—with the extensive pasturelands and the rich farming areas in the Tsangpo Valley represent a major change in the economic geography of Tibet. They facilitate the movement of merchandise between the three cities and the transportation of grain from agricultural areas and livestock products from the pasturelands. The motorable road has reduced travel time between Lhasa and Shigatse from twelve days on foot and yak to two days by car or truck with overnight halt. A nonstop journey would take much less time. The Shigatse-Gyantse highway has had a similar effect. Large truck repair shops have been set up at Lhasa, Gyantse, Gartok, and Sining to service the vehicles using the new highways.

During the last two decades the Chinese have faced a variety of problems resulting from climate and high altitude in keeping the highways open to traffic throughout the year. In addition, guerrilla activities and sabotage in the 1960s interrupted highway construction and hindered traffic flow.

Along with the intensive development of road transport, the Chinese have made significant progress in establishing air service linking Tibet with major centers in China. In May 1956 regular air service was begun between Lhasa and Peking. New landing fields at Khampa Dzong, forty miles north of Sikkim, and at Tingri, north of Mount Everest, were completed in 1959. Additional landing strips near the Ladakh border were built for military aircraft.[55] During 1968–1969 major jet airports were completed near Gyantse and Rudok. By 1970 air transport linked most major centers of Tibet, and Lhasa was serviced by regular flights from Peking, Chungking, and Chamdo.

In 1969 about 20,000 Tibetan and Chinese workers were reported to be completing a major jet airfield south of Shigatse.[56] Tibetan refugee sources indicate that the workers completing the airfield were prison laborers, many of whom died because of harsh climatic conditions at the high altitude and a meager diet of barley powder and black tea. Although Shigatse was the site of sporadic violent clashes between rival Chinese factions in 1969 during the Cultural Revolution, the airfield site was closely sealed off from the town and construction was not affected.

Important achievements have been made in the development of regular navigation for vessels up to 2,000 tons along the Kyi Chu and Tsangpo rivers between Lhasa and Tse-tang. Substantial improvements have also been made in radio and telephone communications. Lhasa, already linked by telephone with Chungking in 1952, was connected with Peking in 1953, and in 1956 this service was supplemented by the establishment of direct radio phone services. A modern communication and postal network connecting Lhasa with Peking, Chungking, Lanchow, Chengtu, Chamdo, Shigatse, and other points has been completed. The Chinese occupation of Tibet depends to a large degree on the maintenance of the modern systems of communications and transport. However, there are still large areas in north and northwest Tibet untouched by modern communications and without firm Chinese control. Many Tibetans have lately escaped from Chinese-controlled areas to join insurgent groups in these remote areas. The Chinese are expected to continue to expand the present network of transportation and communication into remote areas in order to gain complete territorial integration of Tibet with the People's Republic.

54 "Highway Network Linking All Parts of China," *Peking Review* 15, no. 2 (January 14, 1972): 23.
55 *New York Times*, October 15, 1959, p. 9; December 22, 1959, p. 5; December 25, 1959, p. 1.
56 Ibid., December 9, 1969, p. 6.

One major effect of the transportation development has been the reorientation of the flow of Tibetan trade towards China in contravention of the spirit of China's trade agreements with India and Nepal. The policy of isolating Tibet from all foreign influences has made the country an even more strictly quarantined, "forbidden" land than it ever was under the rule of the lamas. For strategic reasons, and perhaps also because the Tibetans are not at all subjugated yet, the process of sealing off Tibet from the rest of the world goes on. But it has its problems for the Chinese.

The main problems are the difficulty of supplying a large Chinese garrison in Tibet and at the same time feeding the local population. Despite the vast road-building program, the routes between Lhasa and China proper are not easy, and Peking is reported to have made it plain that Chinese troops in the autonomous regions such as Tibet must be sustained from local resources. Unfortunately agricultural production in Tibet is barely sufficient for the local population. There is an acute shortage of food grains throughout the country and food is rationed in most towns. The only alternative supply source for the Chinese in Tibet is India, but in view of present Sino-Indian relations that means smuggling. According to one unofficial estimate, about 500,000 tons of Indian food grains, as well as flashlight batteries, kerosene, and road-building implements, now find their way into Tibet through Nepal.[57]

Instances of this smuggling have been raised several times in the Indian Parliament. The Indian states bordering Nepal, mainly Uttar Pradesh and Bihar, have taken measures to police the 500-mile open frontier. But the difficulty of effectively guarding the entire Indo-Nepal border is all to the advantage of the smugglers.

On the return journey, the smugglers bring Chinese-made goods back into India. It is comparatively easy, despite official vigilance, to buy a Chinese-produced fountain pen or cigarette lighter in the open markets of northern India. From the sale of these goods the Chinese get the Indian currency they need for the expenses of their projects in Nepal; they are also reported to be channeling some of the proceeds to the pro-Peking Communists in India, such as the Naxalite group which has seized police and administrative headquarters in various parts of India.[58]

Industrial Development

Handicrafts and artisan type industries were of considerable importance in Tibet before 1951.[59] These traditional enterprises, using mainly the manual labor of family members, included hand spinning and weaving, metalwork, and the making of simple tools and equipment for general use. Among the pastoral Tibetans, the weaving of cloth from yak hair and sheep wool was an important industry. The traditional industries suffered a setback from the exodus of large numbers of artisans following the flight of the Dalai Lama in 1959, the forced departure of many Tibetans to China or to distant work camps, and diversion of raw materials such as wool to China.

Despite these setbacks, reports in the official Chinese press reveal a considerable increase in the output of handicraft industries in Tibet. In Lhasa, Gyantse, and Shigatse, major handicraft centers, the Chinese report rapid growth. In Lhasa alone, the number of handicraft workers increased by over 500 during 1960–1962.[60] The state has provided financial aid to the handicraft workers of Lhasa, Shigatse, and Gyantse to enable them to buy more tools and raw materials.

The development of factories in Tibet under the rule of the lamas was severely hampered by the official policy of isolation and the primitive transportation system. China's attempt to promote the industrial development of Tibet began with a comprehensive survey of the country's natural resources. The scarcity of fuel and power which hampered industrialization was met by the development of coal mines

[57] Washington Post, September 29, 1968.

[58] For China's links with the Naxalites, see Hindustan Standard, September 21, 1969.

[59] Charles Bell, The People of Tibet (Oxford: Clarendon Press, 1928), pp. 100-101.

[60] People's Daily (Peking), June 2, 1962.

and water power resources.[61] In 1956 a 600-kilowatt hydro-electric power plant began to supply power to Lhasa, and in the same year another power plant was completed at Shigatse. A large power station, Naichin hydroelectric plant, was completed in Lhasa in 1960. With the addition of a power generator in 1962 this plant increased Lhasa's electric supply by 25 percent.[62]

In 1971 about a hundred small and medium-sized hydro-electric stations were serving more than half of Tibet's administrative units. The power output in 1970 was reported double that of 1965.[63] In addition to providing power for industry, the development of hydropower stations is changing life on the Tibetan plateau. Electric lights have replaced butter oil lamps in the homes of many peasants and herdsmen, while radio broadcasts loudly announce their progress towards socialist goals.

With the discovery of deposits of iron ore, boron, graphite, and various other minerals, the pace of industrial development in Tibet has been rapid in recent years. The plants and mines opened between 1968 and 1972 are reported to exceed greatly the number established in the previous fifteen years.[64]

Modern industrial development began in the late 1950s with a concentration of plants in central Tibet, where transportation and communications systems were better and there was less danger of sabotage by rebels. In March 1959 a blast furnace with a capacity of one and one-half tons of pig iron, using local ore and coal, was erected at Lhasa. The Wuli coal mine north of Lhasa, discovered and worked by Chinese army personnel, was meeting the fuel needs of the local area. An ordnance factory began producing ammunition in 1964 at a site about two miles east of Lhasa, near the famous Sera monastery, with electricity supplied by the Naichin hydroelectric project on the Kyi Chu.[65]

In addition, a number of small industrial establishments, such as tanneries, canneries, dairies, and other food processing factories, went into operation in the Lhasa suburbs in 1960. A woolen textile mill went into production at Lhasa in 1966. The Lhasa Pharmaceutical Factory produces serum for animals, and the Lhasa Cement Plant, reported to have 400 Tibetan and 100 Chinese workers in 1967, produces building material from locally available coal, clay, sand, and lime.[66] The cement plant is claimed to be producing thousands of tons of high-grade cement each month; previously the Tibetan language had no word for cement. Industrial workers in Tibet numbered 26,000 in 1966. In addition some 8,000 skilled Tibetan workers became qualified lathe turners, fitters, and welders.[67]

A new industrial landscape has grown around Lhasa, Shigatse, and Chamdo during the two decades of Chinese control. The functioning of industrial plants at these centers is largely dependent on Han technicians and workers or members of the People's Army, although the Chinese have successfully trained the first generation of Tibetan workers to handle technical problems independently.[68] New mineral discoveries, continued Han settlement, and improvement of transport facilities will undoubtedly result in further industrial growth in existing centers such as Lhasa, Shigatse, Gyantse, and Chamdo, and may eventually result in the development of new industrial centers close to the sources of raw materials.

Linchih, on the bank of the Nyang River 420 kilometers southeast of Lhasa, is an example of a new center of industrial activity developed since the Cultural Revolution.

[61] "A Coal Mine on the 'Roof of the World,'" *China Pictorial*, no. 6 (1971): 24-25; "Hydropower Stations on the 'Roof of the World,'" *Peking Review* 14, no. 9 (February 26, 1971): 21-22.

[62] New China News Agency, October 27, 1962. Tibet's rivers are reported to have considerable hydroelectric power potential. See "Tibet—Land of Unlimited Potentialities," *Statesman*, December 31, 1965.

[63] Cheng Wen, "Local Industry Advances in Tibet," *Peking Review* 14, no. 29 (July 16, 1971): 22; "More Small Hydroelectric Stations in Minority Nationality Areas," *Peking Review* 14, no. 26 (June 25, 1971): 19.

[64] *Great Changes in Tibet*, p. 38.

[65] *Statesman*, June 2, 1964, p. 6.

[66] "Tibet's Industry Speeds Full Steam Ahead," New China News Agency, Lhasa, December 30, 1966.

[67] "Tibetans Take to Industry," *Times* (London), May 17, 1966, p. 10.

[68] "First Generation of Tibetan Workers Rapidly Maturing," *Peking Review* 13, no. 21 (May 22, 1970): 38.

The technical personnel and workers for this industrial center were sent from Shanghai and other cities in China. With a host of factories producing woolen goods, paper, batteries, and matches, the city is an emerging industrial base. Linchih Woolen Mill, employing more than 1,000 workers, produces fifty types of woolen fabrics, including blankets.[69] The battery plant completed in 1971 reportedly makes Tibet self-sufficient in this product, which used to be brought from China proper.

Industrial production is expected to remain a growing segment of the Tibetan economy under Chinese control. The achievements so far reflect a firm commitment by the Chinese to selective industrial development based on local raw materials and Chinese managerial resources and capital.

[69] Tsang Jen, "Woollen Mill on Tibetan Plateau," *Peking Review* 14, no. 29 (July 16, 1971): 23-24; "The Linchih Woolen Mill," *China Pictorial*, no. 1 (1972): 17.

6

POPULATION CHANGES, REFUGEE MIGRATION & SETTLEMENTS

AT the beginning of the twentieth century Sarat Chandra Das recorded a figure of two and one-half to three million for the male population of all Tibetan territories. Das based his population estimate on the number of monks listed in the Lhasa archives towards the end of the nineteenth century.[1] Earlier, in 1895, William Rockhill had estimated the population of Tibet at three million,[2] and in 1915 David Macdonald estimated the population of the area under the authority of the Dalai Lama at 3.9 million,[3] based on the tax collected by the Lhasa government to repair city's temples. Whatever the validity of such guesses, there seems little question that towards the beginning of the twentieth century, the Tibetan state had a population of over two million. Considering the physical conditions, the limited area of arable land, and the vagaries of climate, this figure may represent the optimum number which Tibet could support within the framework of traditional agriculture and pastoral nomadism.

The 1953 census of China recorded a population of 1,273,969 for Tibet, yet the official Chinese figure for 1951 was 3,750,000. In 1962 the Dalai Lama gave a population figure of "seven or eight million."[4] In view of the wide range of figures, a population of three million may not be far from correct for the present. Hugh Richardson, the former officer-in-charge of the Indian mission in Tibet, favors a figure of three million.[5] The official Chinese figures record a much lower population and also show a decline in population between 1953 and 1959 as indicated in the table on page 53.

According to the New China News Agency release of August 20, 1965, the population of Tibet declined 7.4 percent between 1953 and 1959. This decline was said to be related to the "cruel persecution and oppression" of the population "by the ruling classes," prevalence of epidemic diseases, and feudal conditions. After the "democratic reform" of 1959 leading to the abolition of serfdom a population increase of 1.4 percent was recorded in 1960. Between 1960 and 1965 the population increased 10.4 percent, or an average annual increase of 2.0 percent. Some scholars have questioned this reported annual population growth.[6]

The official explanation of the population change is doctrinaire. Population growth is attributed to the general

[1] Sarat Chandra Das, "Monasteries of Tibet," *Journal of the Asiatic Society of Bengal*, n. s. 1 (1905): 106-16.
[2] William W. Rockhill, *The Ethnology of Tibet*, U.S. National Museum Report, part 2 (Washington, D.C.: Government Printing Office, 1895), p. 674.
[3] David Macdonald, *The Land of the Lamas* (London: Seeley Service Co., 1929), p. 115.
[4] Dalai Lama XIV, *My Land and My People: The Autobiography of His Holiness the Dalai Lama* (New York: Dutton, 1962), p. 200.
[5] *A Short History of Tibet* (New York: Dutton, 1962), p. 6.
[6] Leo A. Orleans, "A Note on Tibet's Population," *China Quarterly*, no. 27 (July/September 1966): 120-22.

Native Population of Tibet, 1953–1965

Year	Population	Source of Data
1953	1,273,969	1953 Census
1957	1,270,000	*Ten Great Years* (Peking: Foreign Languages Press, 1960)
1959	1,180,000	New China News Agency, Lhasa, August 20, 1965
1960	1,197,000	New China News Agency, Lhasa, August 20, 1965
1964	1,270,000	Yu-Ti Jen, *A Concise Geography of China* (Peking: Foreign Languages Press, 1964)
1965	1,321,500	New China News Agency, Lhasa, August 20, 1965

improvements in economic conditions and living standards following the abolition of serfdom in 1959 and the settlement of "homeless serfs" on their own farmland, development of agriculture and livestock breeding, reduction in infant mortality, and expansion of medical facilities, particularly child-care. The development of factories, particularly in Lhasa and Shigatse, is cited as an additional factor.

The Chinese figures given above refer only to the native Tibetan population. They do not include the number of Hans in Tibet. Estimates of the number of Chinese living or stationed in Tibet vary widely. Reports of troop strength vary from 125,000 to 300,000.[7] Chinese-sponsored writers such as Stuart and Roma Gelder have given 40,000 as the total number of Chinese civilians in Tibet; they do not give any figure for the Chinese military population.[8] Based on estimates referred to earlier, a figure of about three million for the total population of Tibet—ethnic Tibetans, new Chinese settlers, civilian Chinese technicians, and military

personnel—may not be too far from the approximate number of people living in Tibet today. There is evidence that China is attempting to bring about a major population increase through a concerted program of resettling Han elements in Tibet. As early as 1952 Mao advocated raising Tibet's population to ten million.[9]

The general pattern of population distribution in Tibet is shown on the map, next page. This pattern is closely related to the river valleys, which represent regions of greater productivity and economic potential. The valleys of southern Tibet which comprise the key economic areas, are: the Tsangpo Valley with a major cluster near Shigatse; the Kyi Chu Valley with the principal cluster around Lhasa; the Mekong Valley near Chamdo; the Upper Indus Valley northwest of Gartok; and a lesser concentration in the Chumbi Valley north of Yatung. Historically, this pattern has shown remarkable stability. These areas of population concentration are regions of intensive land use. The dispersed population clusters, representing oasis-type settlements dependent on irrigation, are separated by large stretches of very sparsely populated areas. The greater part of northern and western Tibet is virtually empty land on the population map. The contrast between small crowded clusters in favorable areas along the southern river valleys and the vast empty lands of the northern interior and plateau is indeed striking. Under Chinese occupation this pattern has intensified with the establishment of Han settlements in areas that were already densely settled.

The population patterns described above have been influenced by a wide variety of interrelated and interacting

[7] George N. Patterson, "Tibet," in *Asia: A Handbook*, ed. Guy Wint (London: Anthony Blond, 1965), p. 114, reports 250,000 Chinese troops stationed in Tibet. Harrison Salisbury, *Orbit of China* (New York: Harper and Row, 1967), p. 104, says 125,000 to 150,000; see also *New York Times*, May 7, 1967, p. 10. *Statesman* (Calcutta), June 2, 1964, estimates 300,000 men. A. H. Stanton Candlin, *Tibet at Bay* (New York: American-Asian Educational Exchange, 1971), p. 52, gives a figure of 250,000 to 300,000.

[8] Stuart and Roma Gelder, *The Timely Rain* (London: Hutchinson, 1964), p. 108.

[9] *New York Times*, November 26, 1952, p. 3.

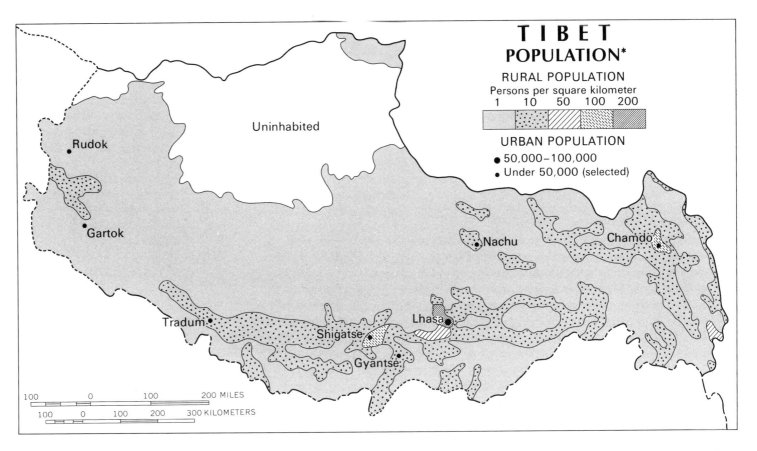

* Generalized pattern based on location of settlements on Survey of India map sheets (1921–1928) updated by information from various sources, including satellite photos.

physical, historical, cultural, and economic factors, and usually there is no simple explanation for the location of a particular settlement or group of settlements. Of all the physical factors which affect the Tibetan population distribution, the availability of water is probably the most significant. Indeed the vital importance of access to water in light of the limited technology of the Tibetan people has meant that few rural settlements are far removed from water sources at or near the surface. Although the location of agricultural settlements may be closely related to water supplies, pastoral settlements are not always so restricted.

Over extensive areas of Tibet the mountainous terrain has

a marked effect on population distribution. Topographic factors, along with the main components of the biogeographic environment such as soils, vegetation, and climate, tend to accentuate the linear pattern of settlement. Historically, there appears to have been a withdrawal of settlement from the really harsh environment of northern and even central Tibet to the river valleys of southern and eastern Tibet, as indicated by numerous abandoned settlements.

The precise influence of historical processes upon the

pattern of population distribution is difficult to trace. Nevertheless some generalizations may be made. Before the advent of Communist China's control, the influence of clan rivalry was of paramount importance. Strong tribal clans afforded security to their members and exploited other people. By means of plunder and the collection of tribute and, in some cases, by trade, some clans were able to strengthen their economy at the expense of others. In this way dominant groups, particularly among the Khampas, built populous settlements which were to some extent dependent upon resources outside their boundaries. On the other hand, the weak groups were generally scattered and their growth was hampered by the depredations of their powerful rival clans. Between the two there developed zones which were usually very sparsely populated.

At least three powerful core areas existed in southeastern Tibet during the second half of the nineteenth century, Chamdo, Lhasa, and Shigatse. Chamdo, in eastern Tibet, located in the area where the great rivers of southeast Asia originate, has been the gateway to China from Tibet. Lhasa, in the Kyi Chu Valley, and Gyantse and Shigatse, along with the valley of the Yarlung, formed the place of origin of the early Tibetan kings. The large population in this cultural and economic ecumene is due in part to the military and political success of the Yarlung dynasty which later formed the nucleus of Tibetan power. The low density of population in areas west and north of this core region may be due partly to their frontier role. The present dense clusters of population at Lhasa, Shigatse, and Gyantse owe much to the development of a highly organized state created by the Tibetan ruling class, whose cultural and political influence extended far into present-day Sikkim, Bhutan, and Nepal, as well as Ladakh, India.

Of all Tibetan tribes, the Khampas were perhaps the most warlike, and the country they occupied reflected their military character. Eastern Tibet, or Kham, with its core area at Chamdo, comprised the dominant political area of the Khampas. This area was encircled by a belt of virtually uninhabited mountain country—the no-man's-land between the powerful and prosperous people and the weaker tribes whom they raided. The large settlements and moderately high population in the valley were appropriate only to victorious, fierce people, relying for at least part of their subsistence on raided crops and beasts produced outside their borders and for the rest on the maximum exploitation of the land within them.

Changes in Lhasa

Among the larger settlements of Tibet, the new Lhasa exhibits vividly the thought and style of life imposed by China. Physically located in the fertile valley through which the Kyi Chu River flows, approximately 12,000 feet above sea level, Lhasa is the world's highest capital city. It is surrounded by high mountains whose slopes are dotted with red and white monasteries clinging precariously to rock cliffs. Dominated by the palace of the Dalai Lama located on the summit of 700-foot Potala Hill rising from the green vale of Lhasa (map, page 56), the old eastern section of the city is a collection of white-washed one- to four-story stone houses along a maze of narrow streets. This older residential area surrounds the Jokhang, the Great Cathedral, which lies in the heart of the old city encircled by Lingkhor road. In 1953 the population of the city was placed at 70,000.[10] Adding the number of people living on the outskirts of Lhasa, in nearby monasteries at Drepung, Sera, and Ganden, and in the new suburbs to the north and west, the population of Lhasa and the environs may now exceed 80,000. The construction of highways linking Lhasa and other Tibetan cities with the economic and population heartland of China in 1954 started a period of rapid population growth. Although the current population figure for Lhasa is not available, the total urban area of Lhasa is now twice the pre-1951 size.[11]

Traditionally, Lhasa's nobility lived in large flat-roofed,

[10] R. R. C. de Crespighy, *China: The Land and Its Peoples* (New York: St. Martin's Press, 1971), p. 122.

[11] Hsin Mao, "Lhasa's New Look," *Great Changes in Tibet* (Peking: Foreign Languages Press, 1972), p. 25.

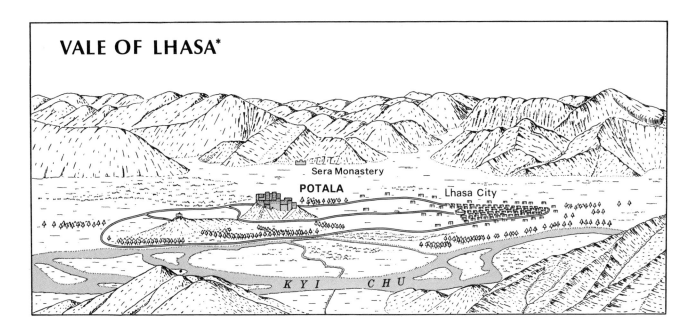

VALE OF LHASA*

Sera Monastery

POTALA

Lhasa City

K Y I   C H U

mud-cemented stone buildings three to four stories high outside the main city. Their comfortable homes were in direct contrast to the homes of the commoners along narrow lanes littered with refuse in the principal residential section of Lhasa east of the Jokhang. A rigorous mountain climate, strong sunshine, and the absence of flies protected the people of Lhasa from the spread of major epidemics in the densely settled part of the city. Since the Chinese occupation this old section of the city has been cleaned and improved sanitary facilities have been constructed.

Between Shargyaring and Thatchen streets to the east of the Jokhang lies the old business area of Lhasa. Containing numerous shops and the residences of shopkeepers, the old Lhasa bazaar until the 1950s featured a wide range of merchandise from China, India, Turkestan, Nepal, and even articles from Europe and America. The fruit and vegetable market and restaurants and cafes line Shargyaring street. Contrary to refugee reports, the Chinese report Lhasa food markets to be stocked with vegetables, beef, mutton, pork,

yak butter, edible vegetable oil, and new foods brought in from China proper, such as bacon from Szechwan and fish from coastal areas. This old business area has declined in importance since 1965 with the development of a new business section in the western part of the city at the foot of the Potala Palace. A new suburb with planned streets and buildings has been developed by the Chinese on formerly marshy land surrounding the Potala. This new suburb contains a shopping area, including bookshops, barbershops, bathhouses, cinemas, and a department store selling woolen fabrics, brightly colored Tibetan aprons, leather boots, aluminum wares, eggs, nuts, fruits, and dry goods. The new shopping area covers 30,000 square meters.

The main street linking the Jokhang and the Potala Palace is flanked by a theater (Happy Light Cinema), radio station, Chinese headquarters, and Chinese transport depot. Lhasa Medical College, where monk doctors have been trained for

* Based on Lhasa map panorama, *National Geographic Magazine,* 1916.

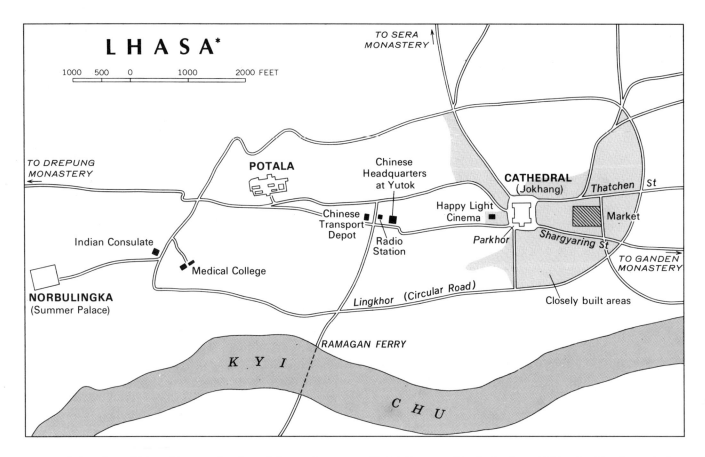

LHASA*

1000 500 0 1000 2000 FEET

TO DREPUNG MONASTERY ←

TO SERA MONASTERY ↑

POTALA

Chinese Headquarters at Yutok

CATHEDRAL (Jokhang)

Thatchen St

Chinese Transport Depot

Happy Light Cinema

Market

Indian Consulate

Radio Station

Parkhor

Shargyaring St

TO GANDEN MONASTERY →

Medical College

Lingkhor (Circular Road)

Closely built areas

NORBULINGKA (Summer Palace)

RAMAGAN FERRY

KYI CHU

years in traditional medicine, lies on the Iron Mountain, a rocky excrescence south of the Potala. The Indian consulate (now closed) and the summer residence of the Dalai Lama, Norbu Lingka are located southwest of the Potala. Surrounded by high walls with several ornamental gateways, Norbu Lingka is nestled among magnificent groves of trees and beautiful gardens.

The Potala Palace, located on Potala Hill, the abode of Chenrezi, the patron saint of Tibet whose incarnation is the Dalai Lama, was completed between 1645 and 1694. Originally constructed by the order of the Fifth Dalai Lama, it served as the traditional winter residence of the succeeding

Dalai Lamas. Until the late 1950s the Potala and the area around it formed the western suburb of Lhasa. The explosive growth of the city to the north and west during the last decade has now made the Potala the center of the city.

During two decades of Chinese occupation, Lhasa has undergone considerable development and modernization. Streets and houses are now lighted with electricity generated by a hydroelectric plant in the neighboring hills. Until 1965 the city had no piped water supply; it now has water pipes serving the residential areas and the various public buildings.

* Base map from Survey of India, Lhasa City (1916). 1:21, 120.

After repairs taking two years, the Potala Palace was reported to have electric lighting and glass windows in 1964. New industries have been completed on the western and northern outskirts. The handicraft workers, who made luxury articles for the nobility, have now formed cooperatives making pumps, forage cutters, soap, and a variety of other products. With the growth of industry and handicrafts, Lhasa has reportedly eliminated its traditional unemployment problem.

In addition to rapid economic improvements, Lhasa has witnessed major progress in education and health services in the last two decades. In 1972 there were thirty-nine primary and secondary schools, with an enrollment of 10,000, run by the government or by factories, people's communes, or neighborhood communities in Lhasa and its outskirts.[12] A stadium, a cultural palace, and theaters have been built which host performances by the revolutionary opera and ballet from China. The people of Lhasa can obtain free health care and treatment at the four modern hospitals and many clinics set up by the Chinese.

With modern transportation links to China the historic isolation of Lhasa has ended. Buses provide regular service with other centers of southern and central Tibet. A modern highway bridge connects Lhasa with a major military base developed across the Kyi Chu River in recent years.[13]

Refugee Migration

Despite modernization and improvements brought about by the Chinese occupation, large numbers of Tibetans (estimated at over 100,000) have fled their homeland. A majority of these refugees are now living in India, with smaller numbers in Nepal and Sikkim. And in recent years Switzerland, Canada, and the United States have admitted small groups of Tibetan immigrants. Of the 56,000 Tibetan refugees who had arrived in India by 1969, 23,000 have been rehabilitated in agriculture, handicrafts, and small-scale industries. The number of Tibetan refugees in India in 1971 was estimated at 100,000 by one source.[14] The government of India plans to rehabilitate the remaining Tibetan refugees

and was spending ten million rupees per year on rehabilitation as of 1970.[15] Some are driving tractors on cooperative farms in tropical South India. Others have learned to quarry limestone, mill paper, or work in other occupations.

Each Tibetan's escape from his country represented a personal triumph over some of the most adverse geographical conditions in the world; it is estimated that two persons died en route for each person who was able to reach a refugee camp in India. The flow was greatest in 1959 when the Dalai Lama's flight triggered an unprecedented migration of freedom-loving Tibetans across the Himalayan passes. As China gradually sealed the passes linking India and Tibet, refugees were forced to cross above the snow line, a formidable task when clothed only in rags. Increased pressure during the 1962 Chinese invasion of India caused a spurt of 20,000 new escapees, severely taxing facilities in India. The flow again slowed to a trickle until the Cultural Revolution. During 1966–1968 hundreds of Tibetans crossed into India to escape the Red Guard movement.[16] In the summer of 1967, after the thawing of snows in the high passes, over 500 Tibetans crossed into the Indian state of Uttar Pradesh. Obviously embarrassed by the mass exodus, China effectively sealed the Indo-Tibetan border adjoining Uttar Pradesh in October 1967, and has also tightened its watch on Tibet's borders with Nepal, Sikkim, and Bhutan. Refugee sources confirm that it has become increasingly difficult to escape. Only the rare refugee or infiltrator now slips through.

In June 1970 there were reports of massive purges in Tibet.[17] Tibetans were being rounded up, made to sign confessions, hauled up before "people's courts" and executed. The mass arrests and executions reflect the new wave of discontent and opposition to Chinese rule.

The Dalai Lama, whose headquarters are in Dharmsala,

[12] Ibid., p. 23.
[13] *Asian Recorder* 16, no. 7 (February 12-18, 1970): 9382.
[14] *Asian Outlook* 6, no. 10 (October 1971): 40.
[15] *India News* (Washington, D.C.: Information Service, Embassy of India), March 20, 1970, p. 4.
[16] *New York Times*, August 28, 1967, p. 1.
[17] *Asian Recorder* 16, no. 29 (July 16-22, 1970): 9648.

India, seeks to maintain morale among the refugee Tibetans and enthusiasm for their ultimate return to their homeland. Some refugees are recruited by the Free Tibetan Movement for missions, including dangerous tasks of infiltrating back into Tibet. Young Tibetans in India now speak Hindi and English, go to movies, respond to trends in fashion, and drift away in small numbers from their traditional ways of life.[18] The Dalai Lama has pointed out that it is up to the refugees to preserve their religion, for it has been systematically stamped out in Tibet.

Chinese propaganda pamphlets being freely circulated to Tibetan refugees in Nepal include a convenient reentry permit to be used at the recipient's convenience. Just in case the point is missed, the good life in Tibet is given special emphasis. How good? No more public floggings, executions, political blackmail, and humiliation. How new? Ever since the Chinese realized what was wrong with the Russian Communist methods they had been using. An excerpt from a speech by a Chinese commander in Tibet illustrates the point: "We admit that there have been in the past many mistakes on the part of our officers. The reason was that because of our good relations with Soviet Russia our policy was chiefly based on the Soviet system of administration, which uses public self-accusations, confiscation of private property, imprisonment, and death penalty for offences. These wrong methods used by us, following the example of the Soviets, have compelled many Tibetans to leave their land and seek refuge in other countries. We have now realized our mistake, and we are sending our old officials for re-education to China. From now onwards we shall free ourselves from the bad influence of the Soviet policy and follow in all matters our own good Chinese Communist ways. With these changes we would welcome the return of all Tibetans who are now in foreign countries."[19]

There seems to be remarkably little enthusiasm among the refugees to use these reentry permits; they may be more eager to return when all the Chinese are back in China learning the new ways. It is clear that the Tibetans dislike for the Chinese Communists (both as Chinese and as Communists) continues to persist. There are more than 10,000 Khampa refugees in the Mustang area of Nepal, where, at an average altitude of 15,000 feet, they evade the tiny Nepalese army. Although there is no evidence that the Khampas now in Nepal or other border areas are slipping into Tibet to resume the fight, Tibetan refugees arriving in India report that guerrilla warfare is still going on intermittently in parts of the country. Tibetan resistance has interrupted the construction of roads and railways and the Chinese have had to resort to air attacks on guerrilla groups.

Refugee Settlements in India[20]

The policy of the Indian government is to set up refugee settlements for the Tibetans in widely separated areas, never too many in one place, to avoid embarrassing concerted political agitation or communal friction. This has presented the Tibetans with problems in their attempts to maintain a government and people in exile. Refugee settlements, all of them agricultural, are located in Mysore, Assam, West Bengal, Madhya Pradesh, and Himachal Pradesh. An estimated 16,000 refugees are still reported unsettled, wandering in bands earning a miserable living as part-time laborers. A small Tibetan settlement has recently been planned in the Ladakh area of Kashmir. Although Ladakh provides a climate and terrain similar to those of Tibet, for political reasons India has been unwilling to allow large numbers of Tibetans to settle there. Most of the 3,000 Tibetans living near Macleodganj in Himachal Pradesh, 6,000 feet up the slopes of the Himalayas, farm the steep slopes, make handicrafts, or sell souvenirs to tourists who make the pilgrimage to "Little Tibet" adjacent to the residence-in-exile of the Dalai Lama. Nearly 1,000 Tibetans are still provided rations

[18] *New York Times*, March 12, 1969, p. 5.
[19] *Statesman* (Calcutta), September 17, 1964.
[20] The sections dealing with refugee settlements were written in 1971. I am grateful to Mr. Phintso Thonden, permanent representative of the Dalai Lama in New York, for information on Tibetan refugee settlements. I visited the refugee settlements in India and the Himalayan countries in summer 1972 and in Europe during July 1973.

of rice, beans, sugar, and potatoes by the Indian government.

An outstanding example of a refugee camp where Tibetans are able to earn a living by their own efforts is the Tibetan Refugee Self-Help Center at Darjeeling, India. Here, nearly 500 Tibetan men, women, and children are educated in Hindi and English and at the same time work to produce Tibetan handicrafts, which are sold in India and exported abroad. Once they have become proficient, refugees move elsewhere to share their skills with others. The camp is ideal, helping Tibetans to help themselves.

A planned settlement for 3,000 Tibetan refugees has been established at Mundgod in Mysore state, South India. Refugees have been settled on 4,000 acres of farm land growing corn and rice. The settlement is divided into six villages. Each village is within a mile or two of another village. Each family of five is accommodated in a three-room brick cottage. The kitchen, bathroom, and cattle yard are detached from the cottage. Each family has been allocated five acres of land, a bullock, and a cow. Seeds and farming implements are made available to them. Until they grow crops in their fields, refugees receive free food and clothing. Organization of the settlement and administration of the villages are supervised by a representative of the Dalai Lama and an officer of the Mysore government.

There is a temple for the entire Tibetan resettlement area in Mysore. For the time being monks receive free rations until settlers can support them. Each village has an elementary school and a community store. Two villages have nursery schools. There is also a dispensary which is planned to be enlarged and converted to a hospital. The refugees settled in Mysore do not have the same environment as in their native Tibet but this fact has not dimmed their ready smiles or tamed their indefatigable spirit.

For several thousand refugees, road-work camps in border areas have proved to be an effective solution to unemployment and have contributed toward raising their morale, but these camps are far from suitable for normal family life. The conditions are necessarily difficult; the life in tents, far from doctors and teachers, is dangerous and unsuitable for the small children. In 1960 the Dalai Lama organized a nursery for Tibetan refugee children at Dharmsala in the Himalayas. When parents in the camps learned that this home for their children had been arranged by the Dalai Lama, they started sending or bringing children of their own accord, and the nursery has now grown far beyond its capacity. Children attending nursery classes learn reading, writing, and arithmetic in their mother tongue and sing the prayers and traditional songs of Tibet. They are also taught Hindi and English. Although help and assistance have come from various quarters, including the Indian government, the problem of young Tibetan refugee children is not resolved—their number is far in excess of the limited capacity of the nursery. Older children are sent to the residential schools in Mussoorie, Simla, and Darjeeling opened by the Tibetan Schools Society working under the auspices of the Indian government.

Refugee Settlements in Nepal, Sikkim, & Bhutan

An estimated 7,000 Tibetan refugees remain in Nepal, most of them along the northern border. A large number of those formerly in Nepal have moved to India. The refugees constitute a major welfare problem, and the government, in cooperation with the International Red Cross, has settled them in groups of 500 in widely separated areas. The largest numbers of groups are around Jumla, Mustang, and Pokhara in western Nepal; in the Khumbu Valley, around Namche Bazar, and in Okhaldhunga in eastern Nepal; and in the Bhairawa district of Western Terai. A few are in the Kathmandu Valley. These concentrations have contributed to grain shortages and rising food prices in some mountain areas. Refugees close to the northern border pose problems for the military and internal security forces. Both anti-communist guerrilla forces and communist agents have reportedly infiltrated the settlements.

There are approximately 4,000 refugees in Bhutan. Most of those arriving from Tibet have moved on to India. Bhutan's

A Tibetan selling his wares in the marketplace in
Gangtok, Sikkim. Many Sikkimese and most Bhutanese
are of Tibetan origin.

Tibetan women living in Gangtok, wearing their
native costume. The style of their jewelry
reflects religious symbolism.

Mother and child, Tibetan refugees in Bhutan.

Above right, Tibetan refugees preparing a meal along
the roadside in Bhutan. Formerly herders in Tibet, they
are employed here in road construction.

Tibetans selling cabbages and reading a Tibetan-language
newspaper in the marketplace in Gangtok.

A refugee mother and child, probably of the Khampa tribe of eastern Tibet.

Lamas at Tihmphu monastery in Bhutan, their hands posed in symbolic Buddhist gestures.

Deorali, a refugee camp for Tibetans in Sikkim. The flags, with prayers written on them, bring good fortune and ward off evil spirits.

A Tibetan woman (in Western-style sweater) lighting incense in front of a chorten in Sikkim.

A Tibetan working at the Refugee Self-help Center in Darjeeling, India.

Courtesy of Press Information Bureau, Government of India.

A Tibetan living in Kalimpong, India, near the Tibetan border. He is holding the traditional prayer wheel and rosary.

Tibetan refugees who have been resettled in Taiwan.
Courtesy of Chinese Information Service, New York.

The Dalai Lama blessing devotees during a visit to Kotah House, New Delhi.
Courtesy of Press Information Bureau, Government of India.

Tibetan refugees now living in Canada. Despite the official policy of assimilation, many attempt to maintain their traditional religion and culture.

Courtesy of Canada Department of Manpower and Immigration, Ottawa.

Tibetan refugees who were employed as lumberjacks in the Maine woods during the early 1960s.

Courtesy of the Great Northern Paper Company, Bangor, Maine.

The Dalai Lama with Pope Paul at the Vatican during a 1974 visit to Europe. Here they exchange a ceremonial scarf.

Courtesy of TIBETAN MESSENGER.

Receiving Tibetan refugees in England during a visit in 1974.

Courtesy of TIBETAN MESSENGER.

policy is to give the refugees the right of transit through Bhutan on the way to India, but to refuse them the privilege of permanent asylum.

Over 7,000 Tibetan refugees fled to Sikkim after the 1959 uprising. Camps and schools were set up and efforts were made to make the refugees self-supporting by employing them in road construction. Only a few were able to accommodate themselves to this kind of work, and India, recognizing their presence as an economic and social burden on Sikkim, moved the bulk of the refugees to Indian camps. The Sikkim Relief and Rehabilitation Committee for Tibetan Refugees, chaired by the sister of the king of Sikkim, has attempted to resettle the remaining refugees in Sikkim. Deorali Camp, near Gangtok, provides facilities for refugees working on roads, and for monks, nuns, the sick, the old, and the infirm.

Sikkim's Enchey School, near Gangtok, offers traditional Tibetan teaching to the children of refugees. Of the present enrollment of over 400 students, nearly 300 are Tibetan refugees. Tibetan studies include grammar, literature, Mahayana Buddhism, and Tibetan astrology. The Enchey School is affiliated with the Central Board of Secondary Education, New Delhi. Expenses of Tibetan students are borne by the Tibetan Schools Society and the Indian government.

Refugee Settlements in Europe

Small groups of Tibetan refugees have been admitted for education and resettlement in various countries of Europe, particularly in Switzerland, where the Tibetan tragedy aroused the natural sympathy of a free alpine people for another mountain people in great need. In 1960 the Swiss Association for Tibetan Homesteads in Switzerland was established to settle groups of Tibetan refugees. In 1961 Switzerland admitted the first group of 23 Tibetans and in 1963 agreed to accept a total of 1,000 refugees. With the goodwill of the Swiss communes and employers, the settlement of Tibetan refugees has met with success.

Over 600 Tibetans have been settled in the area around Rikon. The original plan was to resettle Tibetans in the high mountains where they could find pastoral work in an environment similar to their homeland. But Swiss manufacturers short of labor hired Tibetan refugees. Now there are small communities of Tibetans spread all over German-speaking Switzerland. Ties to the homeland are strongly encouraged and there is now a Tibetan football team called the "Lhasa Boys." In May 1963 a group of Tibetans were settled at Tibeterheim Ennethur (Tibetan Home on the Thur), a large chalet on the hillside above Unterwasser in St. Gallen Canton. Tibetans work as carpenters, market gardeners, laborers, or mill hands. There are now five other Tibetan houses set in the valleys of eastern Switzerland which show how quickly a people traditionally suspicious and distrustful of foreigners can adapt themselves to Western ways. On returning home in the evening, they attend to the religious and Tibetan education of their children. During the day the children, rapidly assimilating Swiss German, take their places in classrooms alongside Swiss children, who in turn have picked up a few Tibetan expressions. The Swiss alpenhorn, echoing occasionally across the valleys, arouses nostalgic memories of a similar instrument once heard amid the high mountains of Tibet. Tibetan children have no time for nostalgia. Switzerland is opening new prospects and they are learning to ski.

In Switzerland, the Tibetan refugees have been hailed for having adapted to a point where they are earning normal wages, have their own homes, and have captured the heart of the country. Their secret of adaptivity has been described as a fine personality rooted in ancient but still living traditions which they continue to practice wherever they go, even while adjusting themselves to changing conditions.[21]

Besides Tibetan resettlers in Switzerland, there are 168 children between the ages of six and seventeen who have been placed in Swiss homes by the Office of Tibet in

[21] Suzanne Oswald, "From Tibet to Switzerland," *Swiss Review of World Affairs*, April 1963, pp. 23-25; "Little Tibet in Switzerland," *National Geographic Magazine* 134 (November 1968): 711-27.

Geneva.[22] In order to keep them informed of their heritage, religion and culture, most of them attend a weekly gathering close to their homes where a Tibetan teacher lectures them in Tibetan and teaches them Tibetan songs, prayers, and language. There are also 41 Tibetan children in the Pestalozzi Children's Village in Trogen, Canton of Appenzell. A few of the children have now passed from the village school and are attending the local higher schools, while a couple of the girls are training for nurses and nurses' aides, and one boy is now receiving agricultural training on a Swiss farm.

There are small groups of Tibetans in France, Germany, the United Kingdom, Belgium, Italy, Norway, and Holland. Twenty Tibetan boys and girls under the supervision of the Ministère des Affaires Etrangères are studying in the Cours d' Enseignement Général in Bléneau, Yonne, France. At the Pestalozzi Children's Village in Wahlwies, Germany, there are fourteen Tibetan children. The Pestalozzi Children's Village in Sedlescombe, Battle, England, houses twenty-two boys and girls. There are five Tibetan boys in Gent, Belgium, and two scholars in Rome. Under the sponsorship of the Tibetanerhjelpen, ten boys are training for different vocations in Norway before they return to India to work in the Tibetan communities. Thirty-two Tibetans have returned to India to work with the Tibetan communities after receiving agricultural training in Norway. There are ten Tibetans in Rotterdam and Leiden, Holland, receiving training for a variety of vocations.

Refugee Settlements in North America

About fifty refugees have settled in the United States assisted by the Tolstoy Foundation, a charitable organization that helps refugees. Founded in 1939 by Alexandra Tolstoy, the daughter of Leo Tolstoy, the organization has also sponsored Tibetan Buddhist monks for study at a Buddhist monastery near Farmingdale, New Jersey.[23]

Six well-educated Tibetan refugees found work in the Maine woods in an experiment designed to curb the labor shortage and to aid displaced persons from far-off lands. The Great Northern Paper Company sponsored the refugees to work in its timberlands in Aroostook County. The Office of Tibet in New York City, which acts as agent for the Tibetan government in exile, made arrangements to bring the refugees to the United States. Although tree harvesting is highly mechanized, there are many areas where the terrain is too rough for the big machines and men still must fell trees by hand. Although the refugees were unfamiliar with woods operations, they were not strangers to hard work in a climate as rigorous as that in Aroostook County. The Great Northern Paper Company reported in 1972 that the Tibetans had accepted other jobs in different parts of the country and were no longer employed by the company.[24]

The mountain states of Idaho, Montana, Wyoming, and Colorado and the northern state of Alaska, where climatic conditions resemble those in Tibet, offer a few areas in North America for resettlement of Tibetans.[25] Of the mountain states Wyoming has the most suitable land for Tibetan settlement: the price per acre is low and there is a shortage of herdsmen. Wyoming ranchers have eased the shortage by importing Basque herdsmen from the Pyrenees Mountains. Their success was attributed to the ability of the Basques to spend long periods on the range far from civilization. Tibetans could easily adapt to the same environment and the same jobs as the Basques.

Although agricultural land is available in Alaska for farming oats, potatoes, and buckwheat to provide the needs of a potential Tibetan refugee settlement, most of the available land is too far from roads and markets, and land closer to

[22] At the request of the Dalai Lama, the Swiss Government authorized the opening of the Tibet Office in 1964 to assist with settlement of Tibetan refugees in Switzerland and other parts of Europe. Mr. Thupten W. Phala, representative of the Dalai Lama in Europe, supplied materials on which this section is based.

[23] *New York Times*, May 3, 1962.

[24] For details of the employment of Tibetan refugees see *New York Times*, July 8, 1967; *Hartford Times*, November 29, 1967.

[25] See David A. McCabe, "Initial Survey of Eventual Possibilities of Tibetan Refugee Migration to the United States," report prepared for the Tolstoy Foundation, New York, August 1964.

centers of population has already been preempted. The Tibetan yak can tolerate the winter conditions of Alaska,[26] and can be slaughtered for meat. Tibetans are familiar with various aspects of yak and yak hybrid husbandry, having used the animals as the mainstay of life in Tibet. With adequate range facilities, a herd of yak and yak hybrids could soon supply ample meat for a Tibetan refugee settlement and later an additional source of meat products for sale in Alaska. In addition, yak hair, currently imported in bulk by the United States, could be delivered more cheaply for its recently developed use as a substitute for human hair in wigs. The principal difficulty with using yak as the backbone of a settlement plan in Alaska is that the majority of yak could graze outdoors only four months of the year and must be fed on ensilage during winter months. Also it might be difficult for the Alaskan public to take to yak meat, since attempts to make reindeer meat popular have not been successful.[27] Not a great deal of beef is raised in Alaska because of competition from grain-fattened steers shipped from Seattle.

Prospects for employment of Tibetans in industry in Alaska also seem dim. Unemployment is high, particularly among Eskimos because of declining activity in the fishing industry. In addition, strong unions are likely to prevent employment of Tibetans and other outsiders in industry unless there is a sudden high demand for unskilled labor. But military activities are no longer expanding and private investment lags. If a limited number of Tibetan refugees could receive enough support for a long enough time to prevent their becoming a burden on the community, the project for a Tibetan settlement in Alaska might have some possibility of success.

The Canadian government has admitted 240 Tibetans on compassionate grounds, but, in accordance with its policy, is not establishing them in separate settlements. They are being trained for occupations in which they will integrate with the general population. The first group, which arrived in the spring of 1971, was settled in a converted mansion in Lindsay, Ontario, just outside Toronto, and in apartments and homes in other Ontario towns.[28] The Tibetans planned to take up factory work after the one-year adjustment period during which they were supported by the Canadian government. Tibetan refugees in Canada are scattered and their children attend local schools in various communities. Because they do not receive education in the Tibetan language and religion, the children may eventually forget the traditions and customs of their ancestors. The new life in Canada is both challenging and rewarding for the Tibetans, but hopefully their culture will not be allowed to disappear.

[26] *Report of the Alaska Agricultural Experiment Station,* (Washington, D.C.: U.S. Department of Agriculture, 1929), p. 19.
[27] See "Reactions in Alaska to Proposed Resettlement of Tibetan Refugees," paper, Tolstoy Foundation, New York, February 1964.
[28] *New York Times,* April 4, 1971, sect. 4, p. 5. For detailed information on groups of Tibetans resettled in Canada see "Tibetans Well Adjusted in Canada," *Tibetan Messenger* (Utrecht, the Netherlands) 2, no. 4 (Winter 1973): 24-26. I am indebted to the Canadian Tibetan Refugee Aid Society for information.

7

THE DESTRUCTION OF TIBETAN CULTURE

THE high plateau of Tibet located between the Kunlun Range in the north and the Himalayas in the south comprises a distinct cultural realm. The arid and mountainous pastoral areas inhabited by nomads, yak-herders, and horse-breeders, and the intensively cultivated agricultural lands settled by peasants in the Tsangpo Valley and Kyi Chu Plain near Lhasa are united by the common bonds of a distinctive culture which finds its significant expression in religion—Mahayana Buddhism. Here for centuries religion pervaded the way of life not only in social and political activities, but also in the system of values, economic organization, land use, material culture, and art forms of this ecclesiastical state.

Huge monasteries, chortens, chapels and temples, stone pillars and mani-walls, all built under religious stimulus, give impressive evidence of the important place of religion in the cultural landscape of Tibet. The large number of monasteries, estimated by one authority to be about 2,500, containing huge populations of monks (760,000 or about a fifth of the total population in 1885)[1] signify the historic supremacy of religion. Built with funds from donors and kept in repair by subscription, the imposing monasteries stand out in the Tibetan landscape with their golden roofs glittering in the sunlight.

For centuries the monasteries trained elites to administer the country. Monastic colleges taught religion, philosophy, astronomy, and grammar and produced books in manuscript or in xylographic block-prints. A great deal of real estate belonged to the monasteries, and most of them amassed great riches from revenues from their estates and community support of liturgical ceremonies. In addition, individual monks and lamas were able to accumulate great wealth through active participation in trade, commerce, and money lending. Generally located in prosperous agricultural areas, or in valleys on the edge of upland grazing areas, in close proximity to most frequented trade routes, monasteries occupied powerful positions in various parts of the country. As the principal institutions for molding intellect, they signified the supremacy of the monastic community.

The monasteries not only exerted powerful religious influences on the political and economic life of the country, but their art and architecture reflect the essential doctrines of Mahayana Buddhism. The architectural style of such monasteries as Samye, built in 775, Drepung, built in 1416, and others follows the model prescribed in Buddhist theology. The chortens and distinctive mani-walls[2] along routes

[1] R. A. Stein, *Tibetan Civilization*, trans. J. E. S. Driver (Stanford: Stanford University Press, 1972), pp. 139-40.

[2] A chorten (cenotaph) may contain the incinerated remains of holy men as well as sacred objects such as images, books, and prayers. Building a chorten was considered a work of the highest spiritual well-being. Chortens are usually located near monasteries, outside towns, and along trade routes. Mani-walls are carved with the six mystic syllables "Om

64

religion, is the very essence of the Tibetan culture. A brief account of the origin of Buddhism in India and its diffusion and development in Tibet is essential to an understanding of the traditional cultural pattern of Tibet.

The Development of Mahayana Buddhism[3]

Buddhists define their religion as the teachings of Gautama Siddhartha, the Buddha (Enlightened One) who preached 2,500 years ago. They accept the Four Truths: 1) suffering is the central fact of life; 2) suffering springs from a cause, that is, it is not an accident; 3) extinction of suffering means escape from the cycle of mortal existence or rebirths (Nirvana); and 4) suffering can be extinguished by human effort, that is by right understanding, right thought, right speech, right action, right livelihood, right effort, right mindfulness, and right concentration.

In addition, all believers accept the Buddha's theory of metempsychosis and believe that one's own Karma, that is, one's deeds and misdeeds, determine one's destiny. They subscribe to a life of nonviolence and fellowship for all life, flowing out of Buddha's crusade against animal sacrifices, to great religious centers are other examples of symbolic representation of Buddhism in the landscape.

Tibetan art reflects the dominant religious element of the culture. Images and tenets of religion form the principal themes in painting and sculpture. Elements of the Tibetan life and landscape such as monasteries, temples, chanting monks, and the traditional white houses appear in Tibetan paintings around images of the motionless, rapt Buddha absorbed in meditative stillness. Dance and dramatic performances concentrate on themes of religious virtue. Literature is dominated by the lives of saints and miracle-workers, and other religious topics. Religious rites dominate birth, death, marriage, and sickness. Tibetans try to protect their homes and occupations through prayers and religious ceremonies. Deities installed at the front corners of a Tibetan house guard it by their divine presence. Special rites are conducted before plowing to insure a good harvest. Cho,

and reject any social distinctions based on birth, as did the Buddha. All pay homage to the Three Jewels—Founder (Buddha), Faith (Dharma), and Fraternity (Sangha)—which are called to witness important political events such as the signing of treaties with other nations.

The differences among schools of practicing Buddhists are in regard to the metaphysical content of the religion and the processes of spiritual striving. Emperor Asoka (ca. 273–32 B.C.), the Constantine of Buddhism, managed to suppress these differences. But by the time of Kanishka (ca. 120 A.D.), Buddhism was divided into the "Great Way" and the "Lesser Way." Those who sought salvation of all beings called themselves Mahayana, the "Great Way" of the Enlightened One, and those who strived for salvation for oneself alone were called Hinayana, the "Lesser Way." The emergence of these two schools of Buddhism in the first century after Christ resulted from an internal development— the discovery of the Secret Teachings of Buddha's dialogues and sermons about the origin and decay of the cosmos which furnished the philosophical basis for the new doctrine of Mahayana. Nagarjuna, a great scholar-monk of South India and probably a contemporary of the Satavahana kings of the South as well as the Kushana kings of the North, who claimed to have discovered the authentic version of the Secret Teachings, is regarded as the father of Mahayana philosophy.

Mahayana spread under Kushana patronage into Inner Asia and China and later into Tibet, Mongolia, Siberia, and Japan. Hinayana prospered in South India, which was outside the Kushana Empire, and later spread into Ceylon, Burma, Thailand, Cambodia, Indonesia, and Malaysia.

Every Buddhist country, whether Mahayana or Hinayana, added its own attitudes and standards in nationalizing the religion. Thus the Buddhism of Tibet or Mongolia differed as much from the Buddhism of China or Japan as Mahayana

---

mani padme hum" ("Oh, Jewel in the Lotus! Amen!") symbolizing the Dharma (truth, law, and religion founded by Buddha).

[3] This section was originally prepared by Professor N. C. Sinha, former director of the Namgyal Institute of Tibetology at Gangtok, Sikkim.

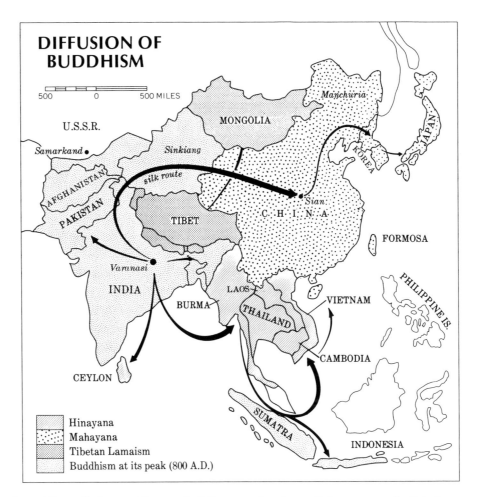

DIFFUSION OF BUDDHISM

500   0   500 MILES

U.S.S.R.

Samarkand •

Sinkiang

silk route

AFGHANISTAN

PAKISTAN

TIBET

Varanasi

INDIA

BURMA

LAOS

THAILAND

CEYLON

SUMATRA

MONGOLIA

Manchuria

KOREA

JAPAN

Sian

CHINA

FORMOSA

VIETNAM

PHILIPPINE IS.

CAMBODIA

INDONESIA

Hinayana
Mahayana
Tibetan Lamaism
Buddhism at its peak (800 A.D.)

did from Hinayana. Overriding all the conflicts and differences was the challenging proposition that everyone could become enlightened like the Great Buddha himself.

The Secret Teachings discovered by Nagarjuna transcended the intellectual limits of public sermons or open teachings and were entitled Transcendental Wisdom (*Prajnâpâramitâ* in Sanskrit, *Sher-chin* in Tibetan). The principal lesson of the Transcendental Wisdom, running through numerous tomes, was that a believer was to strive

for the enlightenment of all beings, not just for his own or that of his friends. In this view liberation from suffering must be universal, for if even a tiny brute is left unredeemed the Nirvana of the rest of the world will be spoiled by the suffering of that lonely brute. A true believer, a Bodhisattva (*Chang-chub sempa* in Tibetan) or a Buddha in the making, should realize that Nirvana is indivisible and thus he must share his piety with his handicapped fellow travellers in the quest for salvation. If necessary a true believer should choose

to be reborn several times; that is, he should undergo the sufferings of mortal life several times so that he can succor to all moral and even material needs of the handicapped ones. Centuries later this ideal of collectivist striving under the leadership of one or more incarnations found a warm reception among the nomadic and pastoral communities in Tibet and Mongolia.

The grand codex of Transcendental Wisdom contained, among its major contents, suggestions for spiritual practices. The aid of supermundane or celestial beings was considered necessary and communion with such beings was found convenient through esoteric rituals. A vast mystic pantheon consisting of Buddhas and Bodhisattvas thus emerged. Nagarjuna and other Mahayana seers were known to be devotees of this mystic pantheon. The mystic element known as Tantra also struck a responsive chord in the Tibetan mind. A Shamanist creed called Bon (Pon) was the native religion of Tibet. This was as ancient as Indian Tantra and the two traditions may have been branches of the same complex, with Mount Kailas overlooking Lake Mansarowar in southern Tibet as the focal point. In India both Brahmanism (Hinduism) and Mahayana openly practiced Tantra. In the Brahmanical code it was called the cult of Power (Sakti) while in the Buddhist code it was called the cult of Thunder (Vajra).

The legendary kings of Tibet came from Magadha (Bihar, in eastern India), the home province of Emperor Asoka (Ny-ngen Me in Tibetan), at a time when Asoka's empire was breaking up. These kings down to the twenty-seventh generation followed the native religion Bon. During the reign of Lha-tho-tho-ri, the twenty-eighth king, a volume of Buddhist canon reached the court; the Kushanas were then ruling over parts of northern India and Inner Asia. The book, when deciphered later, was found to contain the exploits and virtues of the celestial Buddha Avalokitesvara (Chenrezi in Tibetan). As the Lord of Compassion, Avalokitesvara was the leading deity of the Mahayana pantheon. In Tibet he came to be regarded as the father of mankind and adored as the Sole God of the Land of Snow.

Firm evidence about Buddhism in Tibet, however, dates from the time of King Song-tsen-gam-po (ca. 605–650), whose two queens, one from Nepal and one from China, were devout Buddhists. He had a scholarly minister, Thomi Sambhota, who devised an alphabet from Brahmi (Indic) script and founded the systematic translation of the Buddhist canon. Temples were built and images of the Buddha and Mahayana deities were installed. The principal temple was located in the newly founded capital at Lhasa. Monks and scholars from Nepal and India were invited to expound the Buddha's doctrine. The king drew up a code of customs and morals which believers down to the present time have acknowledged and observed as integral parts of the Cho or Dharma. Mahayana eventually became the national religion of Tibet and a dominant feature of Tibetan culture.

The diffusion of Buddhism in Tibet was by no means smooth in the first two centuries, for it had to reckon with the hostility of the native Bon religion. Bon was deeply rooted not only in the mind of the common man but in the court. The Bon priests disputed the authority of the Buddhist monks and challenged them to polemics and mysteries. Victory in doctrinal debates was easy for the scholar-monks who no doubt emphasized the doctrine of salvation for all. The field of magic was, however, not convenient for the monks, as few of them were adept in the occult. In the second half of the eighth century, during the reign of Tri-song De-tsen, the Buddhist monks failed to meet the Bon priests in an encounter of miracle. The Bon elements in the court proclaimed the defeat of Buddhism, which they regarded as a dangerous foreign influence, and reconverted the bulk of the Tibetan population to Bon. The king did not yield, however, and invited the famous Indian master of Tantra, Guru Padmasambhava, to visit Tibet. The guru answered the call, reached Lhasa after overcoming en route the demons set up by the Bon magicians, and in a number of bouts conclusively proved the superiority of his Tantra. For example, he could divert a hailstorm conjured up by the native priests while the native priests could not contain a similar scourge set by the guru. In

short, the superiority of Buddhist magic was indisputable and the Dharma emerged triumphant in the field of mysteries also. Ambivalent believers were soon won over.

The saviour of the Faith came to be adored as Guru Rimpoche (Jewel Teacher or Precious Teacher). Guru Rimpoche was indeed the saviour of Buddhism in Tibet. While his miracles are a matter of belief, his achievements are solid facts of history. Besides proving the superiority of Buddhism over Bon, the guru handled the whole problem of a foreign religion with high statesmanship. He felt the imperative need of nationalizing the church and with the aid of the great philosopher Santarakshita, who was already in Tibet, he ordained the First Seven natives into the Sangha, thereby founding the Lamaist Order. The guru and Santarakshita helped the king to build a monastery on the Tsangpo River, modelled on Odantapuri in Bihar, India, and named after Achintya (Ajanta in western India) as Samye. Above all the guru tolerated some Bon mystic practices which, if not identical with, were not unlike the rituals of Tantra. Buddhism as a universal religion acclimatized itself to the native genius and environment of the country and the guru's cult of Thunder (Vajra) became the national cult of Tibet.

The Chinese exponents of Buddhism who visited Tibet from the time of Song-tsen-gam-po's marriage with a Chinese princess could not comprehend the moral and spiritual needs of Tibetans, whom they referred to as barbarians. A few years after the deaths of Padmasambhava and Santarakshita, two conflicting opinions about the attainment of Enlightenment were being expounded, one by the Indian scholar Kamalasila and the other by the Chinese Hoshang. In a final debate at Samye about 792, the assembly of believers voted for the Indian exponent. Both views, it has since been found, were correct but the Indian master had spoken the Tibetan mind. The Tibetans ceremoniously expelled the Chinese master and banned forever the preaching of Dharma in Tibet by the Chinese. Nearly three centuries later when Atisa came from India to propagate the doctrine, he respected the Tibetan sentiments.

One reason for the success of Buddhism in Tibet was the promise of universal salvation through love, compassion, and the spirit of tolerance. The Mahayana ideal of joint endeavor, in which devotees morally and intellectually superior would share their piety with the handicapped ones, sharpened the edge of Dharma for the nomadic and pastoral communities.

The Red & the Yellow

A common Western usage is to divide Tibetan Buddhism into Red Hat and Yellow Hat, depending on the color of hats worn by the lamas. Red refers to the three earlier sects, Nyingmapa, Kargyupa, and Sakya; Yellow denotes the later Gelugpa sect. The Nyingmapa dates back to the advent of Padmasambhava, that is, the second half of the eighth century; the Kargyupa traces its heritage to a great master of mysticism of eastern India named Naropa (d. 1040); the Sakya, to a scholar and patron of learning from central Tibet named Khon-gyal (1034–1073); and the Gelugpa to a great monk-scholar from Koko Nor named Tsongkhapa (1357–1419). There is a sharp divergence of opinion about esoteric practices and monastic life between the Red sects and the Yellow. For laity in general, however, all temples and monasteries are equally holy and good for both congregation and pilgrimage. Incarnations connected with the Red have been found in Yellow households, while some of the highest Yellow incarnations have come from Red families.

Incarnations: The Dalai & the Panchen

The highest incarnation in the Yellow or Gelugpa sect is the Dalai Lama. The Dalai is the incarnation of Chenrezi, a deity whose compassion is the refuge of all in distress. The third hierarch of the Gelugpa sect, Sonam Gyatso, was called Talai (Dalai) Lama by the Mongol leader Altan Khan, that is, a lama whose virtue was as vast as the ocean, Talai being the Mongol word for ocean. Fourteen hierarchs in succession, each recognized as the manifestation of Chenrezi, are known as the Dalai Lamas of Tibet. The Fifth (Ngawang

Lobzang Gyatso, 1617–1682), the Thirteenth (Thupten Gyatso, 1876–1933), and the Fourteenth (Tenzin Gyatso, born 1935) are regarded as among the great Dalai Lamas.

The Fifth Dalai Lama, the symbol of Tibet's nationalism, unified the country. He visited the Manchu emperor's court in Peking in 1653 and established a patron/priest relationship with the emperor. The Thirteenth Dalai could identify articles belonging to his predecessor when less than two years old and was recognized as the true incarnation in the traditional procedure of omens and rituals ending with his enthronement in 1879. At the time of his death in 1933 Tibet had been completely independent of China for twenty years. He was most anxious to keep foreign powers out of Tibet. When he refused to receive the British emissary in 1903, Britain decided to open Tibet by force. The British Expedition led by Colonel Younghusband reached Lhasa on August 3, 1904, and secured for Britain trading privileges under the treaty of September 7, 1904. Through contacts with Sir Charles Bell, the Thirteenth Dalai Lama acquired a clear image of the outside world and felt the need of reform in government, education, trade, and communications.

Guided by oracles and omens, a search party found the reincarnation of the Thirteenth Dalai Lama in an extraordinary child born on June 6, 1935, in Kumbum. The child passed the identification tests with utmost ease and upon confirmation by the state oracle, the Fourteenth Dalai Lama was consecrated on the Lion Throne of Potala on February 22, 1940. Till the entry of the People's Liberation Army and the Sino-Tibetan agreement of May 23, 1951, the young incarnate functioned as the sovereign ruler of Tibet.

The second highest incarnation in the Yellow sect is the Panchen Lama or Panchen Erteni, the "Precious Scholar"[4] and renowned presiding abbot of Trashi-lhünpo monastery, tutor to the Fourth and Fifth Dalai Lamas. The Fifth Dalai Lama recognized the Panchen as the incarnation of Amitabha (O-pa-me in Tibetan), the primordial Buddha of Limitless Light, the spiritual father of Chenrezi. There have been seven[5] incarnations of Amitabha. The seventh, born

in 1938 in the Koko Nor region of northeastern Tibet which became a part of the Chinese province of Tsinghai, is contemporaneous with the Fourteenth Dalai Lama. Several times in Tibet's history the Chinese have prompted the Panchen Lamas to work for a share in the temporal rule of Tibet.

The Sino-Tibetan treaty of 1951 contained a proviso affirming the status, powers, and functions of the Panchen, and the young reincarnation was brought to Shigatse by the People's Liberation Army and installed in May 1952. The Chinese objective was to establish a counterforce to the authority of the Dalai Lama. After the 1959 uprising in Lhasa and the flight of the Dalai Lama, the Chinese proclaimed the Panchen Lama as the leading "patriotic element" in Tibet and appointed him acting chairman of the Preparatory Committee for the Autonomous Region of Tibet, a position in which he served until his removal from office in 1965.

The Obliteration of Organized Religion

After the 1951 military occupation of Tibet, China faced a political and cultural order pervaded by religion and dominated by the enormous power of the monasteries and feudal estates and of individual monks and lamas. Under the 1951 Sino-Tibetan agreement the People's Republic promised,

[4] Panchen means great scholar in Tibetan, and Erteni means precious in Mongol.

[5] Snellgrove and Richardson consider Lobzang Chokyi Gyaltsen (1570–1662) as the first Panchen Lama. His "reincarnation technically the second Panchen Lama . . . was discovered in 1662 and duly installed." Stein lists ten Panchen Lamas and notes that Khe-Trup (1358–1438) is regarded as the first Panchen Lama by the Tibetans. Richardson explains that the "Higher numbering is the result of calculating that two Abbots of Trashi-lhünpo, before Lobzang Chokyi Gyaltsen, and one of Tsongkapa's disciples were all earlier incarnations of the Panchen Lama," but further comments that according to Tibetan records these three persons are not considered incarnations. He concludes that the higher numbering represents "another way in which champions of the Panchen Lama tried to build up his stature in order to put him more on a level with the Dalai Lama." David Snellgrove and H. E. Richardson, A Cultural History of Tibet (New York: Praeger, 1968), p. 220; Stein, Tibetan Civilization, p. 84; H. E. Richardson, A Short History of Tibet (New York: Dutton, 1962), p. 55.

among other things, to maintain the existing political system of Tibet and to protect freedom of religion and the monasteries. Soon after the establishment of its territorial control, however, China began to violate these promises as it forcefully brought about the "socialist transformation" of Tibet. Cultural associations such as the Young Pioneers and Youth Leagues were organized among Tibetan Buddhists and a serious study of Tibetan religion was made to find out whether Maoism could be interpreted and propagated in terms of the Bodhisattva doctrine.[6] This doctrine, which holds that one who has attained enlightenment remains among the living, refusing salvation in order to help others achieve the same goal, is in practice a sort of "collectivism." But Han attempts to indoctrinate communism through Buddhism failed because of the basic conflict between the communist emphasis on materialism and the Buddhist emphasis on spiritualism, reflected in the Tibetan preference for meditation rather than labor and merit in the next life rather than affluence in the present life.

The systematic and ruthless destruction of Tibetan culture by the Chinese through a variety of methods was exhaustively investigated by a committee of the International Commission of Jurists at Geneva. A report published by the commission in 1960 concluded that China had violated the fundamental rights of the Tibetan people. In relation to Tibetan culture, the report included several specific charges:

Article 16: The voluntary nature of marriage was denied by forcing monks and lamas to marry. . . .

Article 18: Freedom of thought, conscience and religion were denied by acts of genocide against Buddhists in Tibet and by other systematic acts designed to eradicate religious belief in Tibet.

Article 19: Freedom of expression and opinion was denied by the destruction of scriptures. . . .

Article 22: The economic, social and cultural rights indispensable for the dignity and free development of the personality of man were denied. . . . The old culture of Tibet, including its religion, was attacked in an attempt to eradicate it. . . .

Article 26: The right to liberal education primarily in accordance with the choice of parents was denied by compulsory indoctrination, sometimes after deportation, in communist philosophy.

Article 27: The Tibetans were not allowed to participate in the cultural life of their own community, a culture which the Chinese have set out to destroy.[7]

In an earlier report on Chinese policy in Tibet, the commission recorded that "On the basis of the available evidence, it would seem difficult to recall a case in which ruthless suppression of man's essential dignity had been more systematically and efficiently carried out."[8]

The Mimang group reported widespread religious persecutions between 1951 and 1958.[9] These included forcing lamas to abandon their traditional rights to obtain food through charity; torture and starvation of those who would not abandon their faith; forcing monks to build highways, which meant giving up their religious work in temples; forcing monks to marry and then moving them to China to earn a living; levying taxes on the images of Buddha, negating Tibetan spiritual traditions; and forcing lamas into studies of Marxism. In 1959 the Dalai Lama reported that the Chinese had destroyed nearly 1,000 monasteries in eastern Tibet. Chinese attacks on the Potala Palace and the nearby monasteries of Sera, Drepung, and Ganden during the Lhasa uprising led to the destruction of valuable sacred books and records, statues, and paintings, and the death of many lamas and monks. After the uprising, only a handful of lamas and monks were left in monasteries which had formerly housed communities of thousands. Currently,

[6] This is based on information gathered from lamas of Trashi-lhünpo, Drepung, and Sera monasteries now living in Sikkim. For attempts to identify Mao as a Buddha see Holmes Welch, *Buddhism under Mao* (Cambridge, Mass.: Harvard University Press, 1972), p. 291.

[7] International Commission of Jurists, *Tibet and the Chinese People's Republic* (Geneva, 1960).

[8] International Commission of Jurists, *The Question of Tibet and the Rule of Law* (Geneva, 1959), p. 59.

[9] *The Tibet Revolution and the Free World* (Taipei: Asian People's Anti-Communist League, 1959), p. 21.

the Drepung monastery is maintained as a showcase exhibit for foreign dignitaries visiting from Eastern Europe and other communist countries. During the 1967 Cultural Revolution, the Red Guards destroyed the remaining Buddhist images and scrolls in the major temples. Refugee reports confirm that all forms of worship have been abolished since 1968. No more lamas are seen on the streets of Tibetan cities and towns; most of them now work as laborers. The monasteries and temples have been converted into schools and storehouses. The obliteration of organized religion is the most profound transformation wrought by China in the cultural geography of Tibet.

The Role of Education

Before 1951 education in Tibet was the monopoly of the monasteries, which provided training for the elite to lead the country and for ecclesiastical careers. Secular education was nonexistent. Educational policies were viewed first and foremost in light of their bearing on the well-being of religion, which provided the philosophical and theoretical foundation for the educational system.

Soon after the military take-over in 1951, the Chinese launched a campaign to indoctrinate the Tibetan people in Marxism. A radio station and printing presses to turn Marxist literature were established in Lhasa. Cultural and social clubs were organized for use in conjunction with education to remold the views of the Tibetan population. A network of secular public schools was set up. By 1959 the number of schools and cultural organizations established in Tibet was impressive and a large number of Tibetans of all social classes were affected. Their impact was doubtful, however. Many young Tibetans did succumb, but a large number of older conservative Tibetans, particularly the hard core in Lhasa, remained immune to communist endeavors to remold their society and culture. From the outset the monasteries were hostile to the Chinese educational program, and the monks and nobility resented a curriculum designed to destroy the belief of young Tibetans in their

own culture. Until the 1959 uprising Tibetans showed a determined resistance to Chinese efforts at thought control. This situation changed dramatically after the Lhasa uprising and the flight of the Dalai Lama.

During the late 1950s, the large-scale expansion of secular education led to a concomitant decline in the role of the traditional centers of learning, the monasteries and the ecclesiastical community. The extensive system of free primary schools was supplied by books sent from China as well as books and other scholastic materials prepared by the People's Liberation Army in Tibet for free distribution to students. In 1955, there were 27 primary schools with an enrollment of 2,000. In 1956, the number increased to 60, and a comprehensive plan for a public school system was adopted. In the latter year the first secondary school was established in Lhasa. After the 1959 uprising, enrollment in primary schools jumped sharply, exceeding for the first time the capacity of the school buildings. Nearly 5,000 pupils were reportedly enrolled in Lhasa public schools in June 1959, as compared to pre-March enrollment of only 1,000. In February 1960 nearly 150 primary, secondary, and workers' evening schools were operating in all of Tibet. By April 1960, the enrollment in the primary school system had reached 33,000. In Lhasa alone nearly all school-age children were attending classes. In April 1962 the school enrollment was placed at 58,000. By 1965 the total student enrollment had increased to 73,600, with 1,970 primary schools, 7 secondary schools, a teacher's training institute, and an institute for nationalities. Various kinds of evening schools were functioning for emancipated Tibetan serfs, who were reported eager to learn to read and write. The number attending schools in Tibet rose to 83,000 by 1971.[10] The Hungchi commune in the sparsely populated grassland of northern Tibet had established a mobile school with teachers making their rounds to give instruction to all school-age children in the commune. Likewise the herdsmen of Tehchi commune in Nachu had set up 9 primary schools,

[10] "Education in Tibet," Peking Review 15, no. 11 (March 12, 1972): 23.

12 educational centers, and 3 evening classes where students study politics, the three R's, the Tibetan language, and the use of the abacus. Some of the schools in northern Tibet are located at larger settlements. Others are mobile schools housed in tents, serving the children of herdsmen in their own grazing areas. The teachers come regularly to offer instruction, enabling the children to study as well as participate in productive labor.

China's educational program included the establishment of special nationality institutes to indoctrinate students from border regions. The most important among these, the Central Institute for National Minorities in Peking, graduated 210,000 non-Han workers in 1956, including an unknown number of Tibetans. The Institute for Nationalities in Tsinghai offered teacher training in the Tibetan language and provided special training for primary school teachers. The importance of these institutes is reflected in the fact that in 1956–1957 alone the Preparatory Committee sent over 500 young Tibetans for training in the various institutes for nationalities in Peking, Chengtu, and other places in China proper. This program has continued and in 1972 it was reported that "400 workers, peasants and soldiers, most of them sons and daughters of emancipated serfs" had been sent to the Peking Central Institute for Nationalities and other colleges in Shensi province in late November 1971.[11]

Until 1957, the shortage of experienced and ideologically reliable Tibetan personnel at intermediate and lower levels of government was met by bringing in Han administrators from China. But because of the open hostility of the native population towards Han nationals in the mid-1950s, most of them were withdrawn in 1957 and a major program was launched to educate native Tibetans for regional administration. After the 1959 revolt, 1,200 Tibetan graduates of the Central Institute for Nationalities, the Southwest Nationalities Institute, and the Szechwan Public School for Tibetans were repatriated to fill positions in various government agencies.[12] In order to maintain an adequate supply of civil servants of Tibetan origin, the education and training of young Tibetans in China continued vigorously in the 1960s, despite overwhelming public disapproval. Because the vast majority of these Tibetan administrators became members of the Communist Party[13] and were loyal to China's objectives, major cultural changes were made by Tibetans themselves during the 1960s without loss of China's real authority. The introduction of communist-indoctrinated Tibetan administrators paved the way for complete substitution of socialist institutions for traditional elements in all aspects of Tibetan society after the Cultural Revolution.

As a tool for winning the younger generation of Tibetans to the communist value system, the Chinese educational policy has been successful, particularly since the flight of the Dalai Lama. The precise impact on adult Tibetans is difficult to measure. However, it can be said that many adults sent to China's institutes for nationalities acquired only a thin veneer of indoctrination which peeled off when they returned to their homeland, and some joined the rebels as they witnessed the systematic destruction of their religion and culture.

Attempts to Preserve Tibetan Culture

After his flight to India in 1959, the Dalai Lama launched an appeal to the world for the Tibetan people and the preservation of their ancient culture. He felt that the process of integrating exiled Tibetans into the life of their host countries, although essential, should not lead to the wilful destruction of their confidence in the great value of their culture. The pride of Tibetans in their spiritual heritage, their belief in Mahayana Buddhism, and their vivid remembrance of their old home in Inner Asia—all these spiritual values needed protection. Without it, the Tibetans settled in various countries might be swept from their spiritual moorings, and once bewildered and con-

[11] Chao Yang, "Workers, Peasants and Soldiers of Tibet Go to College," *Great Changes in Tibet* (Peking: Foreign Languages Press, 1972), pp. 19-21.

[12] *Survey of China Mainland Press* (American Consulate General, Hong Kong), no. 2075 (August 13, 1959): 37.

[13] Frank Moraes, *The Revolt in Tibet* (New York: Macmillan, 1960), p. 75.

founded by the accomplishments of modern technology and culture they might become rootless proletarians.[14]

With a few notable exceptions the Tibetan refugee settlements in India, Europe, and North America lack proper cultural centers to care for the spiritual and religious needs of the Tibetans in exile, to provide Tibetan scholars and priests with facilities for teaching young compatriots and conveying to them the values of their culture. If they do not preserve their traditions they will no doubt lose their distinctive cultural identity. This is not in the interest of the host countries which, having taken charge of the material well-being of the refugees, are under a moral obligation to look after their religious and cultural needs as well.

In order to keep their ancient faith alive hundreds of Tibetan monks gather each year from refugee camps and settlements all over India for the Dalai Lama's month-long series of seminars on the rites and beliefs of Tibetan Buddhism. Since 1969 the Dalai Lama has held such gatherings in an attempt to pass on the cultural wisdom to his scattered subjects and to a whole new generation of young monks growing up in India with only the dimmest childhood memories of Tibet. Most of the shaven-headed monks in their maroon and saffron robes come from the two Tantric colleges set up for the training of young monks at Dalhousie, India, not far from the Dalai Lama's residence-in-exile. It is too expensive for many to come from refugee settlements of South India and from Sikkim, Bhutan, and Nepal, much less from the Tibetan colonies in Switzerland and Canada. During the annual gathering of monks, the Buddhist temple at Macleodganj in the Himalayas is the scene of much chanting and activity. Four hours every afternoon the Dalai Lama leads his monks in the chants and teaches them from the deep store of his secret knowledge.

The former ruler of Sikkim, with assistance from India and the support of the Dalai Lama, established the Institute of Tibetology in Gangtok, which serves as a repository of Tibetan culture. The cornerstone of the building, which symbolizes the rich and variegated culture of Tibet, was laid by the Dalai Lama and the institute was opened in 1958 by Indian Prime Minister Nehru. The institute's library houses a major collection of ancient books and historical records, many of them donated by the Dalai Lama, dealing with Tibetan religion, art, and history. Lamas of different sects and other scholars at the institute strive to preserve the culture through religious study and research.

At Rumtek monastery, ten miles from Gangtok, Sikkim has offered land and special facilities to the Karmapa Lama, head of the Red Hat Kargyupa sect, and his followers to settle and reestablish themselves. The Karmapa Lama had fled from Tibet through Bhutan, where he has a considerable following, but because of the political risk of an incarnate lama assuming influence in Bhutan, where the institution of Shabdung (spiritual ruler) has been abolished, he settled in Sikkim and endeavors to preserve the traditions of his sect.

As a cultural center for the Tibetans in Europe, the Tibetan Monastic Institute was completed at Rikon, Switzerland, in 1968. The institute, with resident lamas, a spacious place for worship, and a library, was built through contributions by the Swiss people. At present five Tibetan monks led by Abbot Geshe Ugen Teseten attempt to keep the religious and cultural spirit alive among the Tibetans settled in Switzerland.

The Lamaist Buddhist Monastery near Farmingdale, New Jersey, is the only Lamaist establishment in North America which serves as a place for worship and Sunday-school type classes for Buddhists residing in New York, New Jersey, and adjacent areas of Pennsylvania. The monastery was incorporated in 1958 for the preservation of the Buddhist religion and culture. The program of Buddhist teaching and monastic discipline established in the monastery has been approved by the Dalai Lama. Geshe Wangyal, an ordained monk of the famous Drepung monastery near Lhasa, is the founder of the monastery. The Buddhist temple with a number of resident monks and a library of Tibetan works, attempts to preserve the Tibetan tradition in America.

[14] For details see the various reports on Tibetan refugees (1963, 1964, 1966) prepared by the Tolstoy Foundation, New York.

8

THE STRATEGIC IMPLICATIONS OF
THE CHINESE OCCUPATION

For much of recorded history the relationship between Tibet and China has been a complex one. Tibetans and Chinese have at timcs been tied together by a "priest/patron relationship" but have always been pulled apart by ethnic and economic conflicts.[1] In the eighth century Tibetans invaded and conquered parts of China. There were centuries when the Tibetan monks acted as spiritual leaders and teachers of the Chinese rulers. In the eighteenth century the Manchu emperors established a hazy control over the Tibetan plateau, and ambans, Chinese imperial agents, were resident in Lhasa.

In the twentieth century Imperial China and Republican China maneuvered against the Tibetans, against the British, even against the Russians, for sway over Tibet, which all Chinese governments regarded as a vassal.[2] In Lhasa the Dalai Lama turned now to the British, now to the Russians, sometimes even to the Chinese, in order to keep Tibet independent or at least uncontrolled.

Worried by the Communist suppression of Buddhism in neighboring Mongolia during the 1920s and 1930s, the Thirteenth Dalai Lama in 1933, the last year of his earthly existence, warned the Tibetans that "Unless we can guard our own country, it will now happen that the Dalai and Panchen Lamas, the Father and the Son, the Holders of the Faith, the glorious Rebirths, will be broken down and left without a name. . . . the officers of the state, ecclesiastical and secular, will find their lands seized and their property confiscated, and they themselves made to serve their enemies, or wander about the country as beggars do. All beings will be sunk in great hardship and in overpowering fear; the days and the nights will drag on slowly in suffering."[3] Less than two decades after this prophetic statement, Chinese Communist troops entered Tibet, occupied the country, and began to develop it as a major military bastion. The imposition of Chinese rule over Inner Asia established a great

[1] For an analysis of how far pre-1951 Tibet conformed to the pattern of pre-1950 China using constituent elements of culture, see Nirmal Chandra Sinha, *How Chinese Was China's Tibet Region?* (Gangtok: Sikkim Darbar Press, 1967).

[2] For differing views on the international status of Tibet see Alfred Rubin, "The Position of Tibet in International Law," *China Quarterly*, no. 35 (July–Sept. 1968): 110-54; Tieh-tseng Li, *The Historical Status of Tibet* (New York, 1956); idem, "The Legal Position of Tibet," *American Journal of International Law* 50, no. 2 (April 1956): 394-404; Charles H. Alexandrowicz-Alexander, "The Legal Position of Tibet," *American Journal of International Law* 48, no. 2 (April 1954): 265-74; Nirmal Chandra Sinha, *Tibet: Considerations on Inner Asian History* (Calcutta: F. K. L. Mukhopadhyay, 1967), pp. 1-13. For the official Tibetan viewpoint see Government of H. H. the Dalai Lama, *The Internationaol Position of Tibet* (1959; available from the Office of Tibet, 801 Second Avenue, New York, New York 10017). For a short survey of Tibet's relations with China and Britain, see E. T. Williams, "Tibet and Her Neighbors," *University of California Publications, Bureau of International Relations* 3, no. 2 (1937): 99-140.

[3] Sir Charles Bell, *The Portrait of the Dalai Lama* (London: Collins, 1946), p. 380.

land power which has recently shown itself to be vigorously expansive.[4]

The Legal Status of Tibet

The legal position of pre-1951 Tibet is somewhat obscure. No nation ever formally recognized Tibet as a sovereign state although Tibet, Mongolia, and Britain concluded treaties as sovereigns. According to the Chinese, their 1950 military operations in Tibet were a purely domestic affair. On the other hand, Tibet has in fact enjoyed independence from China for the greater part of its history, including the thirty-eight years prior to 1950, that is, from the time the Chinese garrisons were driven out by the Tibetans in 1912. Normally in international practice such a long period of effective independent existence as a nation carries with it de jure recognition. In this case, however, the question of Tibet's international status was wrapped in a cloud of ambiguity owing to the policy of the British government.

Since Britain wished to maintain the actual independence of Tibet as a buffer state between India and China without giving offence to the Chinese Republic, which claimed all the territories of the former Manchu Empire, Sir Henry McMahon, the British plenipotentiary, in 1913–1914 formulated the combination of Tibetan autonomy with Chinese suzerainty—not sovereignty.[5] Since no countries except China, India, Nepal, and Bhutan had common frontiers with Tibet, no other powers were concerned with the matter. The formula worked well enough as long as China was too weak or apathetic to enforce its claim on Tibet by military means. The concept of suzerainty is outmoded, however; in modern times a state either has or has not sovereign rights over a given territory.

Although Tibet was not formally recognized as a sovereign nation, both Great Britain and China clearly acknowledged Tibet's power to enter into treaties with foreign governments in an independent capacity. The Lhasa Convention of 1904, signed by Britain and Tibet without the participation of China but in the presence of the Chinese amban, was an acknowledgement by all parties of Tibet's freedom to con-

duct its affairs. The Anglo-Tibetan Trade Regulations of 1914 were negotiated directly by Britain and Tibet without mention of Chinese supremacy in any way. In 1920 Sir Charles Bell was sent by Britain as its representative at Lhasa,[6] and the diplomatic link remained unbroken until the Chinese occupation. Tibet, not being a part of China, was excluded from the purview of the Chungking Treaty of 1943 by which Britain abrogated all the extraterritorial rights it had enjoyed in the Republic of China. Tibet's eviction of the official Chinese mission from Lhasa in 1912 and the acceptance of passports issued by the Tibetan government as valid international travel documents by India, Great Britain, and the United States gave ample demonstration of Tibet's independent status.

In World War I, Britain received positive and warm support from Tibet, but during World War II, Tibet exercised her sovereignty by remaining neutral.[7] To relieve the strain on the Calcutta-Chungking airlift, American diplomats in 1942 made overtures for supply routes and overland transport of war materials through Tibet.[8] All such proposals were turned down by the monks and aristocrats advising the child incarnation, the Fourteenth Dalai Lama.

Even the 17-Point Agreement of 1951, in word and effect, bears testimony to Tibet's prior independence.[9] If Tibet had

[4] For views of two outstanding American scholars on this topic see Hans J. Morgenthau and Frank N. Trager, "China Is/Is Not an Aggressive Power," *New York Times Magazine*, March 13, 1966, pp. 28-29, 88-92. Morgenthau terms China "a traditional imperialistic power, a great power with great inner strength and natural expansionist tendency" (p. 29); Trager views China's "attempt to get south of the Himalayas . . . as being part of . . . Chinese *drang nach* Southeast Asia" (p. 29).

[5] See H. E. Richardson, *A Short History of Tibet* (New York: Dutton, 1962), pp. 103, 104, 108.

[6] Charles Bell, "Tibet and Her Neighbours," *Pacific Affairs* 10 (December 1937): 428-40.

[7] Nirmal Chandra Sinha, *Tibet: Considerations on Inner Asian History* (Calcutta: F. K. L. Mukhopadhyay, 1967), p. 13.

[8] See Ilia Tolstoy, "Across Tibet from India to China," *National Geographic Magazine* 90, no. 2 (August 1946): 169-222.

[9] See George Ginsburgs and Michael Mathos, *Communist China and Tibet: The First Dozen Years* (The Hague: Martinus Nijhoff, 1964), p. 1. The authors state that "the 17-Point Agreement . . . marked

been a Chinese region like Szechwan or Kansu, there would have been no need for a treaty establishing its incorporation into China; a declaration of its recovery from the K.M.T. and "imperialists" would have marked its "liberation."

Tibet in Asian Geopolitics

The geopolitical role of Tibet in modern times might be said to begin with the first major European military intrusion, that of the British in 1904,[10] which definitely drew Tibet within the ambit of British power politics. From the late eighteenth century, India-based British interests had been widespread over the Tibetan plateau; it is sufficient to recall the missions of Bogle, Turner, and Manning.[11] But with the treaty of 1904, Britain became the dominant power in Tibet in the fullest sense of the word. British rights in Tibet continued unabated until 1947 when they were passed on to India along with its independence.

On the northern flank of Tibet there was an extraordinary overlap of competing Russian and Chinese claims. The great Russian drive to the east in the first half of the eighteenth century had spilled over into Central Asia. By the end of the nineteenth century the Inner Asian margins were firmly under Russian dominance and the Russians held sway over Sinkiang until 1950. After the revolution of 1911, the Chinese authority in Central Asia weakened. It remained for the British to deny Tibet to Russia and to make it an "outer buffer" which then functioned as a de facto sovereign state.

Writing in 1931, Sir Charles Bell, the long-time British representative in Lhasa, noted, "Tibet is of real use to India as a buffer state, and it is in the interest of Britain, as the custodian of India's foreign policy, that Tibet should be strong, independent and free from outside interference, including interference from Britain herself. Tibet is not powerful enough to menace India, even if her peace-loving Buddhists should ever desire to do so. But her mountainous expanses, some sparsely populated, others entirely uninhabited, form an ideal barrier. Thus, since Tibet is very zealous of her independence, her national interest to this extent coincides with that of India and Britain."[12]

When India became independent, she decided to relinquish the extraterritorial rights in Tibet inherited from Britain, since they represented what Nehru termed the "British tradition of imperialism and expansion." In a statement to the Indian Parliament on April 27, 1959, Nehru said: "Being entirely opposed to any such extraterritorial rights in another country, we did not wish to retain them. But in the early days after independence and partition, our hands were full . . . and we had to face very difficult situations in our own country. We ignored . . . Tibet. Not being able to find a suitable person to act as our representative at Lhasa, we allowed for sometime the existing British representative to continue at Lhasa. Later an Indian took his place. Soon after the Chinese armies entered Tibet, the question of these extra-territorial rights was raised and we readily agreed to give them up [in the Sino-Indian Agreement of April 29, 1954]. We would have given them up anyhow, whatever developments might have taken place in Tibet. . . . We placed our relationship with the Tibet region on a new footing."[13]

_____

the end of Tibet's latest forty-year interlude of _de facto_ independence."

[10] Francis Younghusband, _India and Tibet_ (London: John Murray, 1910). For an account of missionaries, merchants, and diplomats who tried to open Tibet, see John MacGregor, _Tibet: A Chronicle of Exploration_ (New York: Praeger, 1970).

[11] See C. R. Markham, ed., _Narratives of the Mission of George Bogle to Tibet, and of the Journey of Thomas Manning to Lhasa_, 2nd ed. (New Delhi: Manjusri, 1971); Samuel Turner, _An Account of an Embassy to the Court of the Teshoo Lama in Tibet_ (London: G. W. Nichol, 1800). See also "Tibet and Great Power Rivalry," in Gavin Hambly, ed., _Central Asia_ (New York: Delacorte Press, 1969), pp. 263-75.

[12] Sir Charles Bell, "Tibet's Position in Asia Today," _Foreign Affairs_ 10 (October 1931): 139.

[13] _Jawaharlal Nehru's Speeches_ 4 (Delhi: Publications Division, Government of India, 1964): 188. India withdrew the military escort stationed at Yatung and Gyantse; handed over to the Chinese the Indian postal, telegraph, and public telephone services in Tibet together with their equipment; gave up twelve Indian government rest houses; and also relinquished buildings in the compound walls of trade agencies at Yatung and Gyantse. See Appendix A for text of treaty. See also C.

Most Indians aware of their country's geography have traditionally regarded the Himalayas as the protection between themselves and the restless movements engulfing Central Asia.[14] But both British strategists and contemporary Indian geopoliticians have looked beyond the mountains to the real historic barrier, the largely unsettled plateau lying between China and the Himalayan passes. K. M. Panikkar, an Indian geopolitician and ambassador to Peking from 1948 to 1952, wrote in 1955 that the fact that the Tibetan plateau had never been organized militarily had been India's great protection. "The fact that the Chinese were unable in the past to organize a strong military area in Tibet should not blind us to such possibilities in the future. It may not be a danger in the immediate future but there is no doubt that an organized modern state in Tibet will alter the character of the Himalayan problem. . . . True, neither the Himalayan passes nor the climate and resources of the country would enable Tibet to threaten seriously the security of its neighbours. No major danger to Indian defenses can develop from a country which is so sparsely populated and whose resources are so meagre. But the Himalayan boundary will be no longer the dead boundary that it has been since the beginning of Indian history."[15]

Panikkar's warning, plain though it was, was made more urgent by the events of the late 1950s. Influenced by the popular slogans of common interests, brotherhood, and coexistence with China, the Indian government failed to take the warnings seriously until the border dispute began in 1959. By then the Chinese were systematically and successfully eliminating some of the factors Panikkar had found hopeful in Tibet—sparse population, meager resources, and lack of organization. In 1960, Panikkar summed up the change in Tibet: "For the first time in history, a great military power in Tibet stretched out its arm to the Himalayan frontiers and the whole area became transformed into something vital and dynamic."[16]

Since 1951 Chinese roadbuilders, technicians, farmers, and soldiers have moved into Tibet and put down roots. The Chinese have carried on one of the most important Han colonization programs in modern history.[17] They plan to bring in as many colonizers as weather and land conditions permit, and the figure could run into several thousand over a period of years. Tibet's climate and geography make it probably the world's least hospitable country, and Chinese settlement plans face difficulty. But so far the colonization has been successful and Tibet's traditional geopolitical role as a sparsely populated buffer zone has vanished.[18] Aware of these developments, several Indian leaders, including Jaya Prakash Narayan, India's prominent socialist statesman, and influential members of the Parliament, called for the restoration of Tibetan independence on the eve of the tenth anniversary of the Tibetan uprising of 1959.[19]

In spring 1973 it was reported that India and China were moving in the direction of normalizing their relations. As a part of this move India was reported to have suppressed the Dalai Lama's annual speech on March 10 marking the fourteenth anniversary of the Tibetan revolt, and to have banned Tibetan demonstrations and celebrations scheduled for the day. The strained relations between the Indian government and the Tibetan exiles caused by these restrictions

---

H. Alexandrowicz-Alexander, "India and the Tibetan Tragedy," *Foreign Affairs* 31, no. 3 (April 1953): 495-500; Dorothy Woodman, *Himalayan Frontiers: A Political Review of British, Chinese, Indian and Russian Rivalries* (New York: Praeger, 1969), pp. 219-24.

[14] For the changing role of the Himalayas in Indian defense see K. M. Panikkar, *The Himalayas in Indian Life* (Bombay: Bharatiya Vidya Bhavan, 1963); idem, "Himalaya and Indian Defence," *India Quarterly* 3 (1947): 127-35, 233-38. For a resume of the Himalayan region as a cultural crossroads see Madanjeet Singh, *Himalayan Art* (Greenwich, Conn.: New York Graphic Society Ltd., 1968), pp. 9-40; and P. P. Karan, "Geographic Regions of the Himalayas," *Bulletin of Tibetology* 3, no. 2 (July 1966): 5-25.

[15] K. M. Panikkar, *Geographical Factors in Indian History* (Bombay, 1955), pp. 54-55.

[16] K. M. Panikkar, *Problems of Indian Defence* (New York: Asia Publishing House, 1960), p. 42.

[17] *New York Times*, November 28, 1956, p. 7; February 6, 1957, p. 10; April 5, 1959, p. 9. Massive Han migration is reported in *Far Eastern Economic Review* 69, no. 34 (August 20, 1970): 14.

[18] Roy Mellor, "The Changing Geographical Value of Tibet," *Scottish Geographical Magazine* 75, no. 2 (September 1959): 113-15.

[19] *Times* (London), March 10, 1969, p. 5.

moved some young Tibetan exile leaders "to launch a mass movement to struggle for the restoration of Tibet's rightful independence." A group of Tibetan militants planned to seek military aid from the Soviet Union and Taiwan to "refuel the guerrilla movement and turn Tibet into China's Vietnam."[20]

Despite these reports the political situation in Tibet as well as the relations between India and China remained unchanged in 1974. The fifteenth anniversary of the Lhasa uprising was celebrated in 1974 at the Mundgod Tibetan settlement in Mysore, India. For the thousands of Tibetans, including the Dalai Lama, who gathered at Mundgod, the future of Tibet was as uncertain as ever.

Tibetan Military Potential

If the vast barrier upland behind the Himalayas provided the most magnificent defense in depth for India in the past, what is its position in the world today? Can Tibet play the same role in the days of air power, rocket artillery, and other revolutionizing factors in the geography of warfare? Can the defense of India be maintained in the face of aircraft which may fly ever higher and ever faster from bases in Tibet? The long-range airplane, the atomic bomb, self-propelled artillery, and other recent inventions within the control of an expansive power on the Tibetan plateau have introduced new factors in the defense of South Asia.

By 1960, Tibet's military potential had been greatly increased by Chinese air power and the development of transport facilities. The Chinese put the Tibetan military bases, communications network, and supply system to good use in their successful drive against India in 1962.[21] The road built through southern Tibet connecting Chamdo, Lhasa, and Shigatse with Gartok, Rudok, and Khotan is designed as much for projecting military power toward countries to the south as for insuring a hold on the non-Han, Moslem Uighur-Kazakh minority. The reopening of the Gilgit-Pamir road through Pakistani-held Kashmir poses a threat to both the Soviet Union and India. In short, the offensive power of Tibetan military bases has been greatly enhanced by

transport development, both surface and air. But if these transportation facilities should be lost the Chinese garrisons could be written off; their containing power would be of little significance. Although modern transportation has altered the tempo and scale of logistics in Tibet, distances, terrain, population, and resources are still of prime importance.

From the twenty-five newly constructed air bases in southern Tibet, such as that at Phari,[22] about five kilometers from the Indian border, China can mount a sustained air attack on India. At present the range of Chinese bombers is about 1,000 miles. That means that from southern Tibet the Gangetic Valley and the northern areas of India and Bangladesh where most of South Asia's industrial and military potential is located can be subjected to sustained attack. However, airpower requires immense ground preparations, and effective and sustained bombing can only be based on a large-scale military administration and considerable industrial potential. The present inability of Chinese power in Tibet to exploit fully the proximity to India can be explained by the lack of adequate industrial development. From the seats of Chinese industrial power, however, manpower and material can be flown to bases in Tibet without interception by hostile forces, and the towns and industries of northern India and Bangladesh may be laid waste if

[20] George Patterson, "The Long Journey Home," *Far Eastern Economic Review* 80, no. 16 (April 23, 1973): 30.

[21] See Samuel B. Griffith, "The Military Potential of China," and V. C. Trivedi, "The Defence of India," in *China and the Peace of Asia*, ed. Alastair Buchan (New York: Praeger, 1965), pp. 65-94, 125-41. China's assault on India via Tibet in 1962 and the construction of strategic military bases and roads along the frontier have been interpreted as an attempt to "weaken India's influence, prestige and economy." See Trivedi, p. 131. For a survey of the communist regime in China from the neighboring countries of India, Sikkim, and the U.S.S.R., see Harrison E. Salisbury, *Orbit of China* (New York: Harper and Row, 1967). See also Drew Middleton, "Red China Reported to Maintain Military Pressure against India," *New York Times*, May 7, 1967, p. 10.

[22] *Asian Recorder* 16, no. 6 (February 5-11, 1970): 9370. See also "India/China: On the Roof of the World," *Far Eastern Economic Review* 83, no. 11 (March 18, 1974): 20.

India's fighter protection fails. But even this may not be easy for the Chinese. Radar, fighter planes, and antiaircraft artillery can provide a strong defense against overwhelming airpower, once the shock of a surprise offense is over.

As to manpower, the simplest and perhaps least adequate measure of modern war potential, the first and most striking fact is the complete mobilization of almost "the entire able bodied population" of southern Tibet, male and female, for tasks in support of the Chinese troops stationed in Tibet.[23] These forces appear to be intended for logistic support for combat troops and use as a casualty corps and as field hospital attendants. About half of the Chinese troops are available for offensive operations, provided the activities of the Tibetan resistance fighters do not increase.

Although to a large extent the Chinese military strength in Tibet is offset by dependence on long-distance transportation from centers of armament production in the east, for limited engagements their supply bases in Tibet are adequate and close to their rear. The Chinese forces moving out from the high Tibetan plateau have to climb only a few thousand feet before reaching the mountain passes and border posts. For their part, Indian forces must struggle upward through mountains from bases a few days' to a week's march away.

Resources in men and materiel, basic as they are to war potential, are in themselves merely latent factors. The decisive factor in a modern war is the preexistence of a technologically advanced base, capable of rapidly retooling itself for military ends. The character and geopolitical situation of the Chinese arsenals which would have to support a military advance from bases in Tibet warrants some discussion. The Chinese industrial growth in Tibet is relatively recent. New industrial developments so far are based on resources which are secondary in scale. There are small iron works at Lhasa and that town is attracting a variety of small engineering industries. But it is unlikely that the war potential of Lhasa's industries will be very significant for some considerable time. In addition, the area, now teeming with military personnel, is far from self-sufficient in food. Since the greater part of Tibet consists of plateau averaging nearly 16,000 feet in altitude, agriculture is possible only in the valleys of the southeast which support the bulk of the country's estimated three million people. Food shortages have provoked riots against the Chinese.[24]

From this brief evaluation of Tibet's military and strategic potential some general conclusions may be drawn. First, Tibet has ceased to be a power vacuum. Its isolation has been decisively broken down. The immense programs of road building, construction of airfields and airstrips, economic development, and Han colonization suggest that the Chinese plan to exploit the strategic advantages which Tibet offers to project their power and influence into South Asia. Although it would still be difficult for massive armies to cross the Himalayas in large numbers and maintain the occupation of territory south of the mountain range, the Chinese have successfully demonstrated that Tibet can be used as the springboard for an attack to threaten Indian defenses along the southern slopes of the Himalayas.

Second, as China's industrial and logistical situation continually improves in Tibet, the strategic advantages which she enjoys by virtue of her position north of the Himalayas will produce growing concern in India and the Himalayan border kingdoms. Nepal is consciously neutralist and Bhutan is openly committed to India but neither is strong enough to develop an independent strategy which would have any chance of enforcing a solution outside the major dichotomy. Yet the existence of these nations does impose some limits on the freedom of action of the major powers.

To summarize, the vast space of the Tibetan plateau north of the Himalayas gave India sufficient protection in the past from cataclysmic changes arising out of either large-scale conquest or great movements of peoples, and preserved the continuity of the Indic religion and social structure. Both politically and militarily the situation has changed now with the establishment of a dynamic power in Tibet. India is open to large-scale bombardment and if the

[23] A. H. Stanton Candlin, *Tibet at Bay* (New York: American-Asian Educational Exchange, 1971), p. 59.
[24] *Far Eastern Economic Review* 71, no. 11 (March 13, 1971): 60.

control of the air should be lost, Indian centers of industry—Calcutta, Jamshedpur, the Bihar-Bengal coal fields—could be pounded out of existence by airborne attack. The entire length of India's Tibetan frontier is exposed.

Another strategic outcome of the Chinese occupation is that Tibet has become an adjunct to the possible military confrontation between China and the Soviet Union. The western part of Tibet is included in the Sinkiang military region, where China and the Soviet Union face each other across a disputed frontier, and western Tibet plays an important role in the defense of Sinkiang, providing additional access routes in the event of hostilities. The ancient northern route to Sinkiang, following the main Silk Road,[25] has occasionally proved insufficient for the rapid movement of soldiers and arms.

In 1963 the Chinese asserted that the Soviet Union had carried out large-scale subversive activities among ethnic minorities in Sinkiang and coerced several thousand Chinese citizens into going to the Soviet Union. Large numbers of Moslem peoples in the Sinkiang area have crossed into the Soviet Union since 1962. As in Tibet, the Chinese have used Han immigration to dilute the strength of Sinkiang's native population. In 1970 it was reported that a "Free Turkestan" movement aimed at "liberating" China's westernmost province had been set up in neighboring Soviet Kazakhstan with the open collaboration of the Soviet authorities.[26] The revolt by ethnic and religious minorities is a source of major trouble for the Chinese in Sinkiang as well as in Tibet.

Sinkiang is a major source of uranium ores and the original site of China's atomic installations. The production of weapons-grade uranium was established there initially with Soviet aid in 1955. Since 1964 the Lop Nor area north of Tibet has been the test site for nuclear weapons. The serious nature of the dispute with the Soviet Union along the Sinkiang border is indicated by the Chinese decision in 1968 to shift some nuclear installations from Lop Nor to a "safer place" in Tibet, apparently in anticipation of a preemptive Soviet air attack. Although the site of the nuclear facilities in Tibet remains unknown, it is reported to be in a valley surrounded by high mountains north of the Himalayas that would be difficult for the Soviets to bomb or hit with missiles.[27]

Although the border has been quiet since the military clashes of early 1969, the tension has deepened and so far all efforts to resolve border disputes have been fruitless.

In addition, near Rudok, in western Tibet, the Chinese have recently deployed 50 to 100 medium-range ballistic missiles with ranges up to 1,500 miles. These missiles, carrying nuclear warheads, are beamed at targets in India to the south and the Soviet Union to the west.[28] These reports perturb India, which successfully exploded a plutonium bomb recently but does not have its own delivery system for nuclear warheads, although the Soviet-supplied surface-to-surface missiles, the Sukhoi-7, and French bombers can deliver India's atomic warheads. Currently, India produces enough plutonium to make thirty-five small bombs per year.[29] The successful explosion of India's nuclear device in 1974 and its rapidly developing nuclear capability have brought about a further shift in the balance of power in Central and South Asia.

[25] The main Silk Road runs between Tun-huang, an oasis town in extreme western Kansu, and Samarkand in Uzbekistan. Feeder roads from the north and south joined it with Mongolia and India (Kashmir). The road was not serviceable during the two Moslem rebellions of the 1860s and 1920s. For details of the road see Sven Hedin, *The Silk Road* (London: Routledge, 1938).

[26] *New York Times*, March 2, 1970, p. 7. See also Alan Jenkins, "Territorial Issues in the Sino-Soviet Conflict," *Tijdschrift voor economische en sociale geografic* 65, no. 1 (1974): 35-47. For Sino-Soviet rivalry and its effects on India see Robert Jackson, "The Great Powers and the Indian Subcontinent," *International Affairs* 49, no. 1 (January 1973): 35-50.

[27] Sydney H. Schanberg, "China Said to Be Moving Nuclear Plant in Tibet," *New York Times*, September 13, 1969, p. 5.

[28] "India/China on the Roof of the World," *Far Eastern Economic Review* 83 (March 18, 1974): 20; see also "Mao's Nuclear Arsenal," *Far Eastern Economic Review* 83 (May 6, 1974): 34.

[29] A Hariharan, "India's 'Peaceful' Atomic Bang," *Far Eastern Economic Review* 83 (May 27, 1974): 14-15.

9

AN ASSESSMENT OF THE COMMUNIST IMPACT

ANY assessment of the record of China's occupation of Tibet is a problem in weighing both methods and material results. Methods have been ruthless, devious, and destructive of traditional human values. The most serious political weaknesses and tensions in Tibet today stem from the means the Chinese have used to establish their communist system and to maintain their power. Material results, on the other hand, have been remarkable. Through controls and pressures, Han authority has forced, and occasionally inspired, the Tibetan masses into economic productivity and social change on a scale unsurpassed in Tibet's history.

In 1951 the Chinese Communists occupied the isolated and remote plateau deeply entrenched in a political, social, and economic pattern developed under the impetus of Lamaist Buddhism. Religion provided the basic cultural and psychological unity among the people of the plateau. There were no highways and much of the plateau was inaccessible. Cities such as Lhasa, Gyantse, and Shigatse were littered with refuse and lacked sanitation. In the countryside, on large estates owned by monasteries and noblemen, agriculture had slumped through centuries of neglect and the failure to make permanent improvements of the cropland by the theocratic feudal owners. Economic backwardness had improverished large sections of the population.

Today, the backwardness and isolation of 1951 have long since vanished. Tibet now produces steel and mines coal.

Lhasa is fast becoming a major industrial center. Chinese factories in Tibet make a wide range of the products of an industrialized economy. Electricity lights the towns, and intensified exploitation of arable land has raised crop yields. In 1973, the Chinese planned, with reasonable prospects of success, to increase substantially the total grain crop of Tibet.

Road mileage has been increased manyfold since 1951. Airlines and telephone links now bind together almost all parts of the plateau, including regions that twenty years ago were accessible only on foot. Old cities such as Lhasa, Chamdo, and Shigatse have increased in population as well as in urbanized area. Scores of places that were only small communities twenty years ago are now thriving settlements and transportation centers. Physical achievements include irrigation works along mountain streams and the generation of hydroelectric power.

Through the work of large numbers of Han settlers from the overpopulated coastal provinces of China, agricultural and industrial developments are creating a new economic growth area in Tibet. From Gartok to Chamdo and from Yatung to Nachu, men are plowing new land, building new factories and roads. Modern communications at the service of a determined central Chinese authority are integrating Tibet into the Han cultural world.

Allowing for communist exaggeration, it is still possible,

on the basis of known facts, to describe Tibet's record of economic growth as remarkable in view of the plateau's former isolation and the low level of technical capability and experience.

Communist China can cite other striking attainments in Tibet. An area that was dominantly illiterate in 1951 now has thousands of students in schools. Hundreds of Tibetan students have been sent to China for advanced education and to learn mechanical skills. They have completed their courses and are back serving as experts in their homeland.

Welfare amenities such as sanitation, housing, and health services have been subordinated, as far as state expenditure is concerned, to capital construction, particularly roads, and agricultural production. But great progress has nevertheless been made in these fields, largely through the mobilization of mass effort. Athletics, popular drama, pamphlets, and magazines—all useful for communist propaganda and increased productivity—have been extensively developed.

Economic production and social reforms are only part of a more fundamental concern with consolidation of Han political domination and the new, all-embracing communist system. This concern has meant uprooting the religious ideas, destroying the privileges of the monks and the nobility, remolding the minds of the Tibetans, establishing the full political-geographical unity of the plateau, and asserting military power and influence over all parts of Tibet.

Communism came to power in Tibet through force, through effective manipulation of the discontent felt by Tibetan peasants, and by exploiting the old rift between the Dalai Lama and the Panchen Lama in spiritual leadership. Its triumph derived, in a sense, from the backwardness of the people and the lack of skillful and articulate leadership that characterized the rule of the Lamas.

The process of communist consolidation of Tibet was both political and military. Red armies swept to the farthest reaches of the plateau and brought unity to the land mass stretching from Sinkiang to western Szechwan. The momentum of the Chinese urge for territorial expansion was contained by the Soviet Union in Central Asia and by India in the Himalayas. The fervor generated by the emergence of a strong Chinese power in Sinkiang and Tibet has been a major factor in China's disputes with the Soviet Union and India.

China sees a close relationship between the maintenance of strong military power and political stability in Tibet. "The Army is the chief component of the political power of the state," Mao Tse-tung has said. During the two decades of communist rule China has carefully nurtured military power and given the People's Army a special role in the administration of the plateau. General Chang Kuo-hua, commander of the Chinese troops that conquered Tibet in 1951, remained in charge of the plateau's administration until 1967 and was a loyal instrument of the Communist Party and its domestic policy. China's military force in Tibet—estimated at five to six acclimatized, well-equipped mountain divisions,[1] plus separate task groups of regimental size, all backed by a semimilitarized adult population providing militiamen—is today a part of the most formidable force in Central Asia. For China it is a principal manifestation of her return to greatness in Inner Asia, an instrument of internal strength, and a defiance of the Soviet Union, which had humiliated the Chinese in Central Asia.

Chinese military forces in Tibet have been used to pioneer, control, and develop the sparsely inhabited and often rebellious border areas; to build networks of irrigation and communications; to harvest grains; and to "tidy up" the communes. It is also an important police and power instrument to help China enforce its political pattern and policies in Tibet.

Communist China has developed Tibet by methods combining great harshness with subtlety and flexibility. The main economic programs and policies have been carried out by a succession of high-pressure campaigns. China has enforced individual and group conformity and obedience by continuous thought control and surveillance.

[1] Franz Schurman and Orville Schell, eds., *Communist China: Revolutionary Reconstruction and International Confrontation, 1949 to the Present* (New York: Vintage Books, 1967), pp. 227-28.

The first great campaign of 1959–1960 linked the distribution of lands to farmers with the liquidation of landlords and all other individuals, including monks and peasants, considered actually or potentially counterrevolutionary. Communist Han cadres aroused groups of Tibetans into vengeful mobs that condemned many monks and members of the nobility to either death, imprisonment, or to the status of propertyless pariahs. In other campaigns, such as those to brainwash young Tibetans, to eliminate religion and indoctrinate the masses, to repudiate old social customs, to build irrigation facilities, to achieve high production targets, to form the communes, the communists have depended less on terror and more on pressure and exhortation. But sentences to forced labor or loss of income are still frequent penalties for Tibetans who do not cooperate. Individuals judged to be engaged in actual counterrevolutionary subversion sometimes still receive death sentences after mass trials.

Twenty-five years after its establishment, the communist regime in Tibet still has no definitive code of laws, no real civil liberties. The government controls occupation, travel, and place of residence; all mass communication media are instruments of propaganda for whatever line the military regime wishes to emphasize at any given time.

The communists have forced Tibetan Buddhists into associations such as the Young Pioneers and the Youth Leagues for indoctrination intended mainly to serve economic production, to facilitate state control, and to secure Chinese authority. Tibetans must affirm their acceptance of Han Communist doctrines and state policies which frequently run directly counter to their faith. The Tibetan people, like other minority groups in "autonomous" areas which cover 60 percent of China's territory and contain many of its mineral deposits, appear to have considerably less real autonomy than the minority groups in the Soviet Union. The Chinese have rapidly wiped out the old beliefs and customs and have divided Tibet into many small communes, ruled as directly from Peking as are any other parts of China. They have put the Tibetan people under constant pressure to subordinate all other loyalties and to acknowledge allegiance only to the Communist Party and Chairman Mao.

In a calculated effort to create a new, loyal, communist-minded generation, the Chinese have given Tibetan youth special attention. With political ideology in command, Tibetans devote themselves first to conformity within the new political and administrative pattern and second to production.

Communist China, for all its military strength, has permanent undertones of weakness in Tibet. The forced pace of economic expansion has prevented any considerable rise in individual living standards. Today, basic foods and clothing are still severely rationed, and the refugees that now occasionally escape into Nepal tell stories of chronic undernourishment, food queues, and a general shortage of goods. The extreme control makes popular revolt unlikely in Tibet. The Chinese Communists are sensitive about all their border areas and have exerted pressure at many points on China's circumference. Undoubtedly, China now regards Bhutan and Nepal as buffer areas of great importance in relation to Tibet, and would probably go to great lengths to prevent any serious military threat to Tibet arising in or from either country. China has also probed the undemarcated southern frontier of Tibet bordering India and has created serious doubts about her intentions regarding the unsettled borders with the Soviet Union.

The key to an understanding of China's transformation of Tibet's land and people must be sought in communist ideological convictions and spatial perceptions. Ideology and imagery clearly mold China's strategy and provide the rationale for both the ends and the means of its policy in Tibet. The Chinese attach extraordinary importance to men's minds and appear to believe that by manipulating them they can bring about a complete socialist transformation of the plateau. The Chinese approach in Tibet combines the standard techniques of the authoritarian state with the characteristic Chinese perception of the political organization of space around China proper. Two main lines of experience have gone into the transformation of Tibet—one

Chinese, one communist. Chinese Communists, during their years of guerrilla activities against the Nationalists, found that small discussion groups were the best way to teach the uneducated peasantry about socialist reforms, the establishment of communes, public health, and literacy. Communist ideology—Maoism—and Chinese persuasion have been fused together in the working mechanism of thought reform in Tibet. Each Tibetan commune is divided into small groups (six to twelve persons) which meet regularly to discuss Mao's teaching, under an elected leader approved by the Chinese authorities. The success of this ideological remolding technique has varied in different segments of the Tibetan population. Among factory workers the ideological indoctrination is generally successful. But the Tibetan farmers, who welcomed some of the material advances, feel that the price, in terms of regimentation and controlled thought, is too high.

The world has watched the Sinicization and harsh ideologically based modernization of a simple people with a distinctive religion and unusual government. The prospect appears bleak that the Chinese occupation will collapse, even with harassment by Khampa guerrillas. So far China has had limited success in remolding Tibetan minds, but striking success in remolding the face of Tibet. If the exiled Dalai Lama and his people ever return to Tibet, they will find it a different place. The old Tibet that fascinated the world for centuries has ceased to exist.

APPENDIXES

A. IMPORTANT TREATIES RELATING TO TIBET

Three treaties, those of 1913, 1951, and 1954, which affirm the independent and special status of Tibet, are printed below. In Article 1 of the 1913 treaty with Mongolia the Dalai Lama recognized the formation of an independent Mongolian state, and in Article 2 the sovereign of Mongolia recognized the formation of an independent state in Tibet. In Article 3 both states promise to take measures for the protection of the Buddhist faith, and in Article 4 mutual assistance against internal and external dangers is promised.

Following the Chinese invasion of Tibet in 1950, a Tibetan mission went to Peking and signed a seventeen-point agreement on May 23, 1951, with the Chinese People's Government. The signing of this agreement marked the end of Tibet's independence. Under the agreement Tibet became an integral part of China and was, in return, assured full regional autonomy. The Chinese government agreed not to interfere with Tibet's political institutions and internal administration.

In the 1954 treaty, India and China reached an agreement on the conduct of trade and commerce between Tibet and India. The Sino-Indian trade agreement offers the world a singular opportunity to study the record of Chinese willingness to abide by the terms of solemnly signed treaties.

TREATY BETWEEN TIBET & MONGOLIA, JANUARY 1913[1]

[Signed at Urga]

Whereas Mongolia and Tibet, having freed themselves from the Manchu dynasty and separated themselves from China, have become independent States, and whereas the two States have always professed one and the same religion, and to the end that their ancient mutual friendships may be strengthened: on the part of the Government of the Sovereign of the Mongolian people—Nikta Biliktu Da Lama Rabdan, acting Minister of Foreign Affairs and Assistant Minister-General and Manlai Caatyr Bei Tzu Damdinsurun; on the part of the Dalai Lama, Ruler of Tibet—Gujir Tsanshib Kanchen Lubsan-Agwan, Denir Agwan Choinzin

[1] H. E. Richardson, *A Short History of Tibet* (New York: Dutton, 1962), pp. 265-67; Sir Charles Bell, *Tibet Past and Present* (Oxford: Clarendon Press, 1924), pp. 150-51.

Tschichamtso, manager of the bank, and Gendun-Galsan, secretary, have agreed on the following:—

ARTICLE 1

The Dalai Lama, Sovereign of Tibet, approves of and acknowledges the formation of an independent Mongolian State, and the proclamation on the 9th day of the 11th month of the year of the Pig, of the master of the Yellow Faith Je-tsun Dampa Lama as the Sovereign of the land.

ARTICLE 2

The Sovereign of the Mongolian people Je-tsun Dampa Lama approves and acknowledges the formation of an independent State and the proclamation of the Dalai Lama as Sovereign of Tibet.

ARTICLE 3

Both States shall take measures, after mutual consideration, for the prosperity of the Buddhist faith.

ARTICLE 4

Both States, the Mongolian and the Tibetan, shall henceforth, for all time, afford each other aid against dangers from without and from within.

ARTICLE 5

Both States, each on its own territory, shall afford mutual aid to their subjects, travelling officially and privately on religious or on State business.

ARTICLE 6

Both States, the Mongolian and the Tibetan, shall, as formerly, carry on mutual trade in the produce of their lands—in goods, cattle, &c., and likewise open industrial institutions.

ARTICLE 7

Henceforth transactions on credit shall be allowed only with the knowledge and permission of official institutions, without such permission no claims shall be examined by Government Institutions.

Should such agreements have been entered into before the conclusion of the present treaty, and should the parties thereto be unable to settle matters amicably, while the loss suffered is great, the payment of such debts may be enforced by the said institutions, but in no case shall the debts concern the Shabinars and Hoshuns.

ARTICLE 8

Should it be necessary to supplement the articles of this treaty, the Mongolian and Tibetan Governments shall appoint special Plenipotentiaries, who shall come to an Agreement according to the circumstances then existing.

ARTICLE 9

The present treaty shall come into force on the date of the signature thereof.

Plenipotentiaries of the Mongolian Government: Acting Ministers of Foreign Affairs Biliktu Da Lama Rabdan and Assistant Minister-General and Manlai Caatyr Bei Tzu Damdinsurun.

Plenipotentiaries of the Dalai Lama, Sovereign of Tibet: Gujir Tsanshib Kanchen Lubsan Agwan, Donir Agwan Choinzin Tschichamtso, manager of the Bank of Tibet, and Gendun-Galsan, secretary.

According to the Mongolian chronology, on the 4th day of the 12th month of the second year of "Him who is exalted by all."

According to the chronology of Tibet, in the year of the Water-Mouse, on the same month and day.

AGREEMENT ON MEASURES FOR THE PEACEFUL LIBERATION OF TIBET[2]

[17-Point Agreement of May 23, 1951]

The Tibetan nationality is one of the nationalities with a long history within the boundaries of China and, like many other nationalities, it has done its glorious duty in the course of the creation and development of the great Motherland. But, over the last 100 years or more, imperialist forces penetrated into China and in consequence also penetrated into the Tibetan region and carried out all kinds of deceptions and provocations. Like previous reactionary Governments, the Kuomintang reactionary Government continued to carry out a policy of oppression and sowing dissension among the nationalities, causing division and disunity among the Tibetan people. The local government of Tibet did not oppose the imperialist deception and provocation and adopted an unpatriotic attitude towards the great Motherland. Under such conditions the Tibetan nationality and people were plunged into the depths of enslavement and sufferings. In 1949 basic victory was achieved on a nation-wide scale in the Chinese people's war of liberation; the common domestic enemy of all nationalities—the Kuomintang reactionary Government—was overthrown and the common foreign enemy of all nationalities—the aggressive imperialist forces—was driven out. On this basis the founding of the People's Republic of China (CPR) and of the Chinese People's Government (CPG) was announced.

In accordance with the Common Programme passed by the Chinese People's Political Consultative Conference (CPPCC), the CPG declared that all nationalities within the boundaries of the CPR are equal and that they shall establish unity and mutual aid and opposed imperialism and their own public enemies, so that the CPR will become a big family of fraternity and cooperation, composed of all its nationalities. Within the big family of all nationalities of the CPR, national regional autonomy shall be exercised in areas where national minorities shall have freedom to develop their spoken and written languages and to preserve or reform their customs, habits and religious beliefs, and the CPG shall assist all national minorities to develop their political, economic, cultural and educational construction work. Since then, all nationalities within the country—with the exception of those in the areas of Tibet and Taiwan—have gained liberation. Under the unified leadership of the CPG and the direct leadership of higher levels of people's governments, all national minorities have fully enjoyed the right of national equality and have exercised, or are exercising, national regional autonomy.

In order that the influences of aggressive imperialist forces in Tibet might be successfully eliminated, the unification of the territory and sovereignty of the CPR accomplished, and national defence safeguarded; in order that the Tibetan nationality and people might be freed and return to the big family of the CPR to enjoy the same rights of national equality as all other nationalities in the country and develop their political, economic, cultural and educational work, the CPG, when it ordered the People's Liberation Army (PLA) to march into Tibet, notified the local government of Tibet to send delegates to the central authorities to conduct talks for the conclusion of an agreement on measures for the peaceful liberation of Tibet. In the latter part of April 1951 the delegates with full powers of the local government of Tibet arrived in Peking. The CPG appointed representatives with full powers of the local government of Tibet. As a result of the talks both parties agreed to establish this agreement and ensure that it be carried into effect.

(1) The Tibetan people shall unite and drive out imperialist aggressive forces from Tibet; the Tibetan people shall return to the big family of the Motherland—the People's Republic of China.

(2) The local government of Tibet shall actively assist the PLA to enter Tibet and consolidate the national defences.

[2] Richardson, *Short History*, pp. 275-78.

(3) In accordance with the policy towards nationalities laid down in the Common Programme of the CPPCC, the Tibetan people have the right of exercising national regional autonomy under the unified leadership of the CPG.

(4) The central authorities will not alter the existing political system in Tibet. The central authorities also will not alter the established status, functions and powers of the Dalai Lama. Officials of various ranks shall hold office as usual.

(5) The established status, functions and powers of the Panchen Ngoerhtehni shall be maintained.

(6) By the established status, functions and powers of the Dalai Lama and of the Panchen Ngoerhtehni are meant the status, functions and powers of the thirteenth Dalai Lama and of the ninth Panchen Ngoerhtehni when they were in friendly and amicable relations with each other.

(7) The policy of freedom of religious belief laid down in the Common Programme of the CPPCC shall be carried out. The religious beliefs, customs and habits of the Tibetan people shall be respected and lama monasteries shall be protected. The central authorities will not effect a change in the income of the monasteries.

(8) Tibetan troops shall be reorganised step by step into the PLA and become a part of the national defence forces of the CPR.

(9) The spoken and written language and school education of the Tibetan nationality shall be developed step by step in accordance with the actual conditions in Tibet.

(10) Tibetan agriculture, livestock-raising, industry and commerce shall be developed step by step and the people's livelihood shall be improved step by step in accordance with the actual conditions in Tibet.

(11) In matters related to various reforms in Tibet, there will be no compulsion on the part of the central authorities. The local government of Tibet should carry out reforms of its own accord, and, when the people raise demands for reform, they shall be settled by means of consultation with the leading personnel of Tibet.

(12) In so far as former pro-imperialist and pro-Kuomin-tang officials resolutely sever relations with imperialism and the Kuomintang and do not engage in sabotage or resistance, they may continue to hold office irrespective of their past.

(13) The PLA entering Tibet shall abide by all the above-mentioned policies and shall also be fair in all buying and selling and shall not arbitrarily take a needle or thread from the people.

(14) The CPG shall have centralised handling of all external affairs of the area of Tibet; and there will be peaceful co-existence with neighbouring countries and establishment and development of fair commercial and trading relations with them on the basis of equality, mutual benefit and mutual respect for territory and sovereignty.

(15) In order to ensure the implementation of this agreement, the CPG shall set up a Military and Administrative Committee and a Military Area HQ in Tibet and—apart from the personnel sent there by the CPG—shall absorb as many local Tibetan personnel as possible to take part in the work. Local Tibetan personnel taking part in the Military and Administrative Committee may include patriotic elements from the local government of Tibet, various districts and various principal monasteries; the name-list shall be set forth after consultation between the representatives designated by the CPG and various quarters concerned and shall be submitted to the CPG for appointment.

(16) Funds needed by the Military and Administrative Committee, the Military Area HQ and the PLA entering Tibet shall be provided by the CPG. The local government of Tibet should assist the PLA in the purchase and transport of food, fodder and other daily necessities.

(17) This agreement shall come into force immediately after signature and seals are affixed to it.

Signed and sealed by delegates of the CPG with full powers: Chief Delegate—Li Wei-Han (Chairman of the Commission of Nationalities Affairs); Delegates—Chang Ching-wu, Chang Kuo-hua, Sun Chih-yuan. Delegates with full powers of the local government of Tibet: Chief Delegate—Kaloon Ngabou Ngawang Jigme (Ngabo Shape); Delegates—Dazasak Khemey Sonam Wangdi, Khentrung

Thupten Tenthar, Khenchung Thupten Lekmuun, Rimshi Samposey Tenzin Thundup. Peking, 23rd May 1951.

AGREEMENT BETWEEN THE REPUBLIC OF INDIA AND THE PEOPLE'S REPUBLIC OF CHINA ON TRADE AND INTERCOURSE BETWEEN TIBET REGION OF CHINA AND INDIA[3]

[Sino-Indian Agreement, April 29, 1954]

The Government of the Republic of India and the Central People's Government of the People's Republic of China.

Being desirous of promoting trade and cultural intercourse between Tibet Region of China and India and of facilitating pilgrimage and travel by the peoples of China and India.

Have resolved to enter into the present Agreement based on the following principles:

(1) mutual respect of each other's territorial integrity and sovereignty,

(2) mutual non-aggression,

(3) mutual non-interference in each other's internal affairs,

(4) equality and mutual benefit, and

(5) peaceful co-existence.

And for this purpose have appointed as their respective Plenipotentiaries:

The Government of the Republic of India, H. E. Nedyam Raghavan, Ambassador Extraordinary and Plenipotentiary of India accredited to the People's Republic of China; the Central People's Government of the People's Republic of China, H. E. Chang Han-fu, Vice-Minister of Foreign Affairs of the Central People's Government, who, having examined each other's credentials and finding them in good and due form, have agreed upon the following:—

ARTICLE I

The High Contracting Parties mutually agree to establish Trade Agencies:

(1) The Government of India agrees that the Government of China may establish Trade Agencies at New Delhi, Calcutta and Kalimpong.

(2) The Government of China agrees that the Government of India may establish Trade Agencies at Yatung, Gyantse and Gartok.

The Trade Agencies of both Parties shall be accorded the same status and same treatment. The Trade Agents of both Parties shall enjoy freedom from arrest while exercising their functions, and shall enjoy in respect of themselves, their wives and children who are dependent on them for livelihood freedom from search.

The Trade Agencies of both Parties shall enjoy the privileges and immunities for couriers, mail-bags and communications in code.

ARTICLE II

The High Contracting Parties agree that traders of both countries known to be customarily and specifically engaged in trade between Tibet Region of China and India may trade at the following places:

(1) The Government of China agrees to specify (1) Yatung, (2) Gyantse and (3) Phari as markets for trade. The Government of India agrees that trade may be carried on in India, including places like (1) Kalimpong, (2) Siliguri and (3) Calcutta, according to customary practice.

(2) The Government of China agrees to specify (1) Gartok, (2) Pulanchung (Taklakot), (3) Gyanima-Khargo, (4) Gyanima-Chakra, (5) Ramura, (6) Dongbra, (7) Puling-Sumdo, (8) Nabra, (9) Shangtse and (10) Tashigong as markets for trade; the Government of India agrees that in future, when in accordance with the development and need

[3] Government of India, Ministry of External Affairs, *White Paper* 1 (Delhi, 1961), pp. 98-101.

of trade between the Ari District of Tibet Region of China and India, it has become necessary to specify markets for trade in the corresponding district in India adjacent to the Ari District of Tibet Region of China, it will be prepared to consider on the basis equality and reciprocity to do so.

ARTICLE III

The High Contracting Parties agree that pilgrimage by religious believers of the two countries shall be carried on in accordance with the following provisions:—

(1) Pilgrims from India of Lamaist, Hindu and Buddhist faiths may visit Kang Rimpoche (Kailas) and Mavam Tso (Manasarovar) in Tibet Region of China in accordance with custom.

(2) Pilgrims from Tibet Region of China of Lamaist and Buddhist faiths may visit Banaras, Sarnath, Gaya and Sanchi in India in accordance with custom.

(3) Pilgrims customarily visiting Lhasa may continue to do so in accordance with custom.

ARTICLE IV

Traders and pilgrims of both countries may travel by the following passes and route:

(1) Shipki La pass, (2) Mana pass, (3) Niti pass, (4) Kungri Bingri pass, (5) Darma pass, and (6) Lipu Lekh pass.

Also, the customary route leading to Tashigong along the valley of the Shangatsangpu (Indus) River may continue to be traversed in accordance with custom.

ARTICLE V

For travelling across the border, the High Contracting Parties agree that diplomatic personnel, officials and nationals of the two countries shall hold passports issued by their own respective countries and visaed by the other Party except as provided in Paragraphs 1, 2, 3 and 4 of this Article.

(1) Traders of both countries known to be customarily and specifically engaged in trade between Tibet Region of China and India, their wives and children who are dependent on them for livelihood and their attendants will be allowed entry for purposes of trade into India or Tibet Region of China, as the case may be, in accordance with custom on the production of certificates duly issued by the local government of their own country or by its duly authorised agents and examined by the border check-posts of the other Party.

(2) Inhabitants of the border districts of the two countries who cross the border to carry on petty trade or to visit friends and relatives may proceed to the border districts of the other Party as they have customarily done heretofore and need not be restricted to the passes and route specified in Article IV above and shall not be required to hold passports, visas or permits.

(3) Porters and mule-team drivers of the two countries who cross the border to perform necessary transportation services need not hold passports issued by their own country, but shall only hold certificates good for a definite period of time (three months, half a year or one year) duly issued by the local government of their own country or by its duly authorised agents and produce them for registration at the border checkposts of the other Party.

(4) Pilgrims of both countries need not carry documents of certification but shall register at the border checkposts of the other Party and receive a permit for pilgrimage.

(5) Notwithstanding the provisions of the foregoing paragraphs of this Article, either Government may refuse entry to any particular person.

(6) Persons who enter the territory of the other Party in accordance with the foregoing paragraphs of this Article may stay within its territory only after complying with the procedures specified by the other Party.

ARTICLE VI

The present Agreement shall come into effect upon ratification by both Governments and shall remain in force for

eight (8) years. Extension of the present Agreement may be negotiated by the two Parties if either Party requests for it six (6) months prior to the expiry of the Agreement and the request is agreed to by the other Party.

Done in duplicate in Peking on the twenty-ninth day of April, 1954, in the Hindi, Chinese and English languages, all texts being equally valid.

[Sd.] Nedyam Raghavan
    Plenipotentiary of the
    Government of the
    Republic of India

[Sd.] Chang Han-fu
    Plenipotentiary of the
    Central People's
    Government, People's
    Republic of China

NOTE
Peking, April 29, 1954

Your Excellency Mr. Vice-Foreign Minister,

In the course of our discussions regarding the Agreement on Trade and Intercourse Between the Tibet Region of China and India, which has been happily concluded today, the Delegation of the Government of the Republic of India and the Delegation of the Government of the People's Republic of China agreed that certain matters be regulated by an exchange of Notes. In pursuance of this understanding, it is hereby agreed between the two Governments as follows:—

(1) The Government of India will be pleased to withdraw completely within six (6) months from date of exchange of the present notes the military escorts now stationed at Yatung and Gyantse in Tibet Region of China. The Government of China will render facilities and assistance in such withdrawal.

(2) The Government of India will be pleased to hand over to the Government of China at a reasonable price the postal, telegraph and public telephone services together with their equipment operated by the Government of India in Tibet Region of China. The concrete measures in this regard will be decided upon through further negotiations between the Indian Embassy in China and the Foreign Ministry of China, which shall start immediately after the exchange of the present notes.

(3) The Government of India will be pleased to hand over to the Government of China at a reasonable price the twelve (12) rest houses of the Government of India in Tibet Region of China. The concrete measures in this regard will be decided upon through further negotiations between the Indian Embassy in China and the Foreign Ministry of China, which shall start immediately after the exchange of the present notes. The Government of China agrees that they shall continue as rest houses.

(4) The Government of China agrees that all buildings within the compound walls of the Trade Agencies of the Government of India at Yatung and Gyantse in Tibet Region of China may be retained by the Government of India. The Government of India may continue to lease the land within its Agency compound walls from the Chinese side. And the Government of India agrees that the Trade Agencies of the Government of China at Kalimpong and Calcutta may lease lands from the Indian side for the use of the Agencies and construct buildings thereon. The Government of China will render every possible assistance for housing the Indian Trade Agency at Gartok. The Government of India will also render every possible assistance for housing the Chinese Trade Agency at New Delhi.

(5) The Government of India will be pleased to return to the Government of China all lands used or occupied by the Government of India other than the lands within its Trade Agency compound walls at Yatung.

If there are godowns and buildings of the Government of India on the above-mentioned lands used or occupied and to be returned by the Government of India and if Indian traders have stores, godowns or buildings on the above-mentioned lands so that there is a need to continue leasing lands, the Government of China agrees to sign contracts

with the Government of India or Indian traders, as the case may be, for leasing to them those parts of the land occupied by the said godowns, buildings or stores and pertaining thereto.

(6) The Trade Agents of both Parties may, in accordance with the laws and regulations of the local governments, have access to their nationals involved in civil or criminal cases.

(7) The Trade Agents and traders of both countries may hire employees in the locality.

(8) The hospitals of the India Trade Agencies at Gyantse and Yatung will continue to serve personnel of the Indian Trade Agencies.

(9) Each Government shall protect the person and property of the traders and pilgrims of the other country.

(10) The Government of China agrees, so far as possible, to construct rest houses for the use of pilgrims along the route from Pulan-chung (Taklakot) to Kang Rimpoche (Kailas) and Mavam Tso (Manasarovar); and the Government of India agrees to place all possible facilities in India at the disposal of pilgrims.

(11) Traders and pilgrims of both countries shall have the facility of hiring means of transportation at normal and reasonable rates.

(12) The three Trade Agencies of each Party may function throughout the year.

(13) Traders of each country may rent buildings and godowns in accordance with local regulations in places under the jurisdiction of the other Party.

(14) Traders of both countries may carry on normal trade in accordance with local regulations at places as provided in Article II of the Agreement.

(15) Disputes between traders of both countries over debts and claims shall be handled in accordance with local laws and regulations.

On behalf of the Government of the Republic of India I hereby agree that the present Note along with Your Excellency's reply shall become an agreement between our two Governments which shall come into force upon the exchange of the present Notes.

I avail myself of this opportunity to express to your Excellency Mr. Vice-Foreign Minister, the assurances of my highest consideration.

His Excellency	[Sd.] N. Raghavan
Mr. Chang Han-fu	Ambassador
Vice-Minister of	Extraordinary and
Foreign Affairs	Plenipotentiary of the
Central People's	Republic of India
Government, People's	
Republic of China	

B. THE DALAI LAMAS

The Dalai Lamas, heads of the Gelugpa Sect and the incarnations of Chenrezi (Avalokitesvara) have been rulers of Tibet since 1391.[1]

I	Gedun-trup	1391–1474
II	Gedun Gyatso	1475–1543
III	Sonam Gyatso	1543–1588
IV	Yonten Gyatso	1589–1617
V	Ngawang Lobzang Gyatso	1617–1682
VI	Tsangyang Gyatso	1683–1706
VII	Kesang Gyatso	1708–1757
VIII	Jampel Gyatso	1758–1805
IX	Luntok Gyatso	1806–1815
X	Tshultrim Gyatso	1816–1837
XI	Khedrup Gyatso	1838–1856
XII	Trinle Gyatso	1856–1875
XIII	Thupten Gyatso	1876–1933
XIV	Tenzin Gyatso	6 June, 1935–

[1] The dates refer to the years of birth and death of the Dalai Lamas. Some of the dates are controversial. For example, Tucci gives 1933 as the year in which the Thirteenth Dalai Lama died; others such as Snellgrove and Richardson say 1934. See Giuseppe Tucci, *Tibet: Land of Snows* (New York: Stein and Day, 1967), p. 31; David Snellgrove and H. E. Richardson, *A Cultural History of Tibet* (New York: Praeger, 1968), p. 276.

C. THE HISTORICAL DEVELOPMENT OF TIBET, CA. 605-1975

Early Kings

600[1]   Yarlung King establishes nucleus of Tibetan state.

605–650   Under rule of Song-tsen-gam-po Tibet becomes imperial power. Diffusion of Mahayana Buddhism.

763   Sian, China's capital, captured by Tibet.

822   Treaty signed between Tibet and T'ang dynasty of China.

842–1100   Tibetan kingdom breaks up into a number of feudal and monastic principalities.

Ascendency of Sakya Sect & Mongol Overlordship

1100–1200   Monastic centers dominate Tibetan society and political institutions.

1200–1350   Grand Lamas of Sakya Sect become rulers of Tibet under Mongol overlordship.

1368   Fall of Mongol dynasty in China. Tibet becomes independent of China.

1350–1400   Sakya Grand Lamas lose political power.

Hierarchs of Gelugpa Sect & Restoration of Independence

1391–1474   Gedun-trup, first Dalai Lama.

1475   Second Dalai Lama born.

1500   Gelugpa Sect (Yellow Hat) firmly establishes itself in Tibet.

1570–1662   First Panchen Lama.[2]

1578   Third Hierarch of Gelugpa Sect, Sonam Gyatso, given title of Dalai Lama by Mongol leader Altan Khan.[3]

Dalai Lamas—Kings of Tibet

1642   Gushri Khan, leader of Qosot Mongols, declares Dalai Lama sovereign ruler of Tibet.

1653   Dalai Lama visits Peking.

1716   Italian priest, Ippolito Desideri, reaches Lhasa.

Manchu Authority Established in Tibet

1720   Manchu Emperor establishes authority over Tibet.

1728   Chinese representatives (ambans) established at Lhasa.

1775   Warren Hastings, governor general of East India Company territories in India, dispatches George Bogle for mission to Tibet.

1850   Manchu authority in Tibet declines.

1888   Clash between Great Britain and Tibet in Sikkim.

1904   Sir Francis Younghusband, leader of British expedition to Tibet, arrives in Lhasa. Treaty between Britain and Tibet.

[1] Some of the dates given in this table are approximate. Further research is needed to authenticate precise dates.

[2] See chapter 7, note 5, above.

[3] Although Sonam Gyatso was properly the first Dalai Lama, the title is traditionally also applied to his two predecessors.

Restoration of Tibetan Independence

1911   Manchu Dynasty ends in China.

1912   Tibet declares independence. Chinese are evicted from Tibet.

1913   Tibet and Mongolia sign treaty.

1914–1918 Tibet lends support to Britain during World War I.

1935   Fourteenth Dalai Lama born.

1939–1945 Tibet remains neutral during World War II.

1942   President Roosevelt sends Lt. Col. Ilia Tolstoy and Capt. Brooke Dolan to Lhasa under auspices of Office of Strategic Services.

1947   Indian mission takes over responsibilities of Britain in Tibet.

Communist Occupation of Tibet

1950   October 7: Chinese invasion of Tibet begins. October 19: Chamdo falls to Chinese. December: Tibet appeals to United Nations.

1951   May 23: Sino-Tibetan agreement signed. Tibet loses independence. Chinese occupy most of Tibet.

1954   Sino-Indian agreement with regard to Tibet signed. Dalai Lama visits China.

1955   Preparatory Committee for Autonomous Region of Tibet inaugurated.

1956   Guerrilla activities against Chinese begin.

1958   Chinese determination to dominate Tibet results in further tension and discontent.

1959   March: Lhasa uprising. March 17: Dalai Lama leaves Lhasa for exile in India; April 18: reaches Tezpur, Assam, India.

1960–1966 Socialist transformation of Tibet accelerates.

1965   Panchen Lama removed from office. Nagbo Nawang Jigme named head of newly proclaimed Autonomous Region of Tibet.

1966–1968 Cultural Revolution marked by extensive destruction of Buddhist monasteries. August 25, 1966: Red Guards sack Jokhang, main temple of Lhasa.

1967   General Chang Kuo-hua transferred to Szechwan. Tseng Yung-ya appointed commander of Tibet Military Region.

1968   Tseng Yung-ya named chairman of Tibetan Revolutionary Committee.

1969   Panchen Lama disappears; reported dead in Chinese prison.

1971   Jen Jung replaces Tseng Yung-ya on Revolutionary Committee. Tseng disappears from public scene.

1972   Dalai Lama offers to return to Tibet on condition the Chinese hold internationally supervised plebiscite on future of Tibet.

1973   October–November: Dalai Lama makes first trip of any Dalai Lama to West, visits eleven European countries.

1974   Dalai Lama goes to Mundgod Tibetan settlement in Mysore for New Year's Prayer Festival and March 10 Commemoration of Lhasa uprising. Plans pilgrimage to Buddhist sites in Soviet Union.

        Khampas use Nepalese territory as base for guerrilla attacks on the Chinese in Tibet.

1975   Broadcasts from Tibet urge their refugees to return.

SELECTED BIBLIOGRAPHY

Works cited here represent a cross section of recent writings essential to the understanding of modern Tibet. The selection focuses on the more readily accessible publications, but even within these limits it does not attempt to be comprehensive. With a few exceptions, this bibliography omits works published before 1950, some of which are important. Many volumes listed below include bibliographies which more fully cover publications available in particular fields. There is a general bibliographic survey by B. D. Miller, "A Selective Survey of Literature on Tibet," *American Political Science Review* 47 (December 1953): 1135-51. A more comprehensive list of publications on Tibet, mainly in European languages, is found in Sibadas Chaudhuri, *Bibliography of Tibetan Studies* (New York: International Publications Service, 1973). A major bibliography covering not simply the usual historical items but virtually every aspect of Tibetan life and civilization is by E. Gene Smith, *University of Washington Tibetan Catalogue* (Seattle: University of Washington Press, 1969). Chinese and Soviet scholars are doing excellent work on Tibet, but much of it appears in sources which are not readily available.

The transcripts of official news items and radio broadcasts relating to Tibet provide useful information on economic, social, and political developments. These items are available in volumes entitled *Survey of China Mainland Press* and *Selections from China Mainland Magazines* (American Consulate General, Hong Kong); and *Daily Report: Chinese People's Republic*, until July 1971 entitled *Communist China* (Foreign Broadcast Information Service, Washington, D.C.). All of these materials can be obtained from the National Technical Information Service, U.S. Department of Commerce, Springfield, Virginia 22151.

Map References

Geographers will find the Survey of India large-scale maps (1:253,440), published at various dates, a most useful source of information on vegetation, land use, and the cultural landscape. These maps are restricted in India, but older editions may be consulted at the Library of Congress in Washington, D.C., and in London at the Royal Geographical Society and the British Museum. The U.S. Army Topographic Command has published general map sheets of Tibet (1:250,000) which are useful sources of information. For Tibetan place names as approved by the United States Board on Geographic Names see *Place Names in Tibet* (Washington, D.C.: U.S. Board on Geographic Names [Division list no. 4515], 1945); and U.S. Office of Geography, *Hong Kong, Macao, Sinkiang and Tibet: Official Standard Names Approved by the U.S. Board on Geographic Names* (Washington, D.C.: Government Printing Office, 1955).

General References

John MacGregor, *Tibet: A Chronicle of Exploration* (New York: Praeger, 1970), gives an interesting and exciting review of the travel of missionaries, merchants, and diplomats. From the meticulous journals of these travelers came the early descriptions of Tibet, its people, and its religion. Several of these early reports have been reprinted recently in India and the United States.

The British expedition to Lhasa in 1904, described by Peter Fleming in *Bayonets to Lhasa: The First Full Account of the British Invasion of Tibet in 1904* (New York: Harper, 1961) was followed by several significant works on Tibet by writers such as Edmund Candler, *The Unveiling of Lhasa* (London: Arnold, 1905); Sir Thomas Holdich, *Tibet, the Mysterious* (London: Alston Rivers, 1906); Perceval Landon, *Lhasa: An Account of the Country and People of Central Tibet and the Progress of the Mission Sent There by the English Government in the Year 1903–4* (London: Hurst and Blackett, 1906); Sir Francis Younghusband, *India and Tibet: A History of the Relations between the Two Coun-*

tries from the Time of Warren Hastings to 1910, with a Particular Account of the Mission to Lhasa of 1904 (London: Murray, 1910; reprinted in Delhi: Oriental Publishers, 1971); L. A. Waddell, *Lhasa and Its Mysteries* (London: Murray, 1905); and others.

Most volumes on Tibet appearing during the first half of the twentieth century were either of a specialized scholarly nature or general travel accounts. The occupation of Tibet in 1951 by Communist China resulted in several papers on political and historical aspects of the region in scholarly journals. However, geographic studies of recent economic and cultural changes in the Tibetan landscape are largely lacking. The most useful single volume analyzing these changes is by George Ginsburgs and Michael Mathos, *Communist China and Tibet: The First Dozen Years* (The Hague: Martinus Nijhoff, 1964).

The Tibetan revolt against the Chinese in 1959 and the subsequent flight of the Dalai Lama and thousands of Tibetans into exile have resulted in a flash flood of publications, ranging from biographies, such as the autobiography of the brother of the Dalai Lama, Thubten Jigme Norbu, *Tibet Is My Country* (New York: Dutton, 1961), and of the Fourteenth Dalai Lama, *My Land and My People: The Autobiography of His Holiness the Dalai Lama* (New York: Dutton, 1962), to general surveys of Tibetan history and culture going back to ancient times, such as H. E. Richardson, *A Short History of Tibet* (New York: Dutton, 1962). David Snellgrove and H. E. Richardson, *A Cultural History of Tibet* (New York: Praeger, 1968) is the best introduction to the rich intellectual and cultural heritage of Tibet. For those who wish to go into detail, Tsepon W. D. Shakabpa, *Tibet: A Political History* (New Haven: Yale University Press, 1967) is valuable but poorly arranged and hard for the reader seeking a clear concept of the thrust of Tibetan history.

Among books which interpret the historical and political factors that led to the 1959 revolt are Frank Moraes, *The Revolt in Tibet* (New York: Macmillan, 1960); George N. Patterson, *Tibet in Revolt* (London: Faber and Faber, 1960); and Lowell Thomas, Jr., *The Silent War in Tibet* (New York: Doubleday, 1959). Noël Barber, *From the Land of Lost Content: The Dalai Lama's Fight for Tibet* (Boston: Houghton Mifflin, 1970) provides a moving picture of seven weeks of anguish and violence as they were lived by residents of Lhasa during the 1959 uprising.

Tibet, 1950–1967 (Hong Kong: Union Research Institute, 1968) is a volume of great reference value containing 189 Chinese and Tibetan documentary source materials on a variety of subjects, including the accomplishments of the Chinese Communist leadership in Tibet, the "Constitution of Tibet" promulgated by the Dalai Lama on March 10, 1963, and the accusations and counteraccusations that characterized the Cultural Revolution and the activities of the Red Guards in Tibet. *Facts about Tibet, 1961–65* (n.d.) was published and compiled by the Bureau of His Holiness the Dalai Lama in India and contains useful statistical information.

Among the periodicals, *Tibet Society Bulletin* and *Tibet Society Newsletter* (Bloomington, Indiana), *Tibetan Review* (monthly, Darjeeling, India), *Tibetan Messenger* (Utrecht, the Netherlands), and *Bulletin of the Namgyal Institute of Tibetology* (Gangtok, Sikkim) are devoted exclusively to Tibetan affairs. Despite some unevenness, *Tibetan Review*, *Tibet Society Bulletin* and *Newsletter*, and *Tibetan Messenger* contain articles of value and much information of interest to geographers. The *Bulletin* of the Namgyal Institute publishes specialized scholarly papers, largely on the history and culture of Tibetan lands.

The student of Tibetan affairs cannot neglect several classic works, including those of Sir Charles Bell, *Tibet: Past and Present* (Oxford: Clarendon Press, 1924); *The People of Tibet* (Oxford: Clarendon Press, 1928); and *The Portrait of the Dalai Lama* (London: Collins, 1946); Sarat Chandra Das, *Journey to Lhasa and Central Tibet*, ed. W. W. Rockhill (New Delhi: Manjusri Publishing House, 1970; first published in 1902); and Sven Anders Hedin, *Trans-Himalaya: Discoveries and Adventures in Tibet* (New York: Greenwood Press, 1968).

Tibetan Literature

The bulk of Tibetan literature is of a religious character covering a broad range of related topics including history, culture, and art. There is much of interest here to scholars of the cultural and historical geography of Tibet. For a general discussion see A. I. Vostrikov, *Tibetan Historical Literature*, translated from the Russian by Harish Chandra Gupta; Indian Studies, Past and Present (Calcutta, 1970).

The voluminous literature crystallized around Padmasambhava, the great apostle from Swat (now in Pakistan) who was consequential in establishing Lamaism in Tibet during the eighth century, and the poems and legends of Milarepa provide eloquent observations and reflections on the theme of nature and the role of perception and mental images and myths in the shaping of Tibetan civilization. For a collection of Milarepa's poems see W. Y. Evans-Wentz, *Tibet's Great Yogi Milarepa*, 2nd ed. (New York: Oxford University Press, 1969), and J. Bacot, *Le Poète Tibetain Milarepa* (Paris: Fayard, 1971).

Collections of the personal writings of the Dalai Lamas, the Panchen Lamas, and high church dignitaries, and of folk songs provide a magnificent interpretation of the Tibetan landscape and the basic attributes of the Tibetan social structure and value system. Giuseppe Tucci, *Tibetan Folk Songs from Gyantse and Western Tibet*, 2nd ed. (Anscona, Switzerland: Artibus Asiae Publishers, 1966) is an excellent source book.

The great collection of volumes popularly known as the *Kanjur*, comprising the utterances of Buddha and the adopted canon of the sacred writings of Buddhism translated into Tibetan from the original Sanskrit texts by Buddhist monks, form a basic source for understanding Tibetan attitudes. The Tibetan translations are almost literal and are prepared with great care and accuracy. Because most of the Sanskrit originals are lost, they are of rich potential interest for the cultural geographer. An English edition is Lokesh Chandra, ed., *The Collected Works of Bu-ston* (New Delhi: International Academy of Indian Culture, 1965).

The different sectarian editions of the *Kanjur*, varying in content, illustrations, and arrangement, are valuable in interpreting the development of Tibetan life and institutions. Each sectarian edition has had a long and varied history, having been translated, corrected, revised, reedited, and commented upon several times. A critical comparison of the various editions of the *Kanjur*, the literary history of which is recorded in their deeply probing prefatory comments, would provide interesting materials on the historical geography of the major Buddhist sects of the plateau. Some of these materials are available in the library of the Namgyal Institute of Tibetology at Gangtok, Sikkim, and in the library of Tibetan works and archives at Dharmsala, India. The latter is described in "Library of Tibetan Works and Archives at Dharmsala," *American Library* 4 (November 1973): 598.

For the convenience of readers who may wish to pursue further studies of certain aspects of Tibet, references have been grouped below under specific topics. Such distinctions cannot, of course, be clear-cut and there is often a measure of overlap between various subjects.

Physical Environment

Chia Shen-hsiu. "Natural Conditions of Tibetan Plateau." *K'o Hsueh T'ung Pao* [Science Bulletin] (Peking), August 1953, pp. 51-58.

Chong Ching-wei. "The Basic Characteristics and the Zonal Significance of the Grassland in the Southeastern Part of Ch'iang-t'ang Plateau." *Chih-wu Sheng-t'ai-hsueh Yu Ti-Chih Wu-Ts'ung-K'an* [Plant Morphology and Phytogeography] (Peking), 1, nos. 1-2 (1963): 131-40.

Chung Pu-ch'iu. "Vegetation and Its Distribution Conditions in Tibetan Plateau." *Sheng Wu Hsueh T'ung Pao* [Biological Bulletin] (Peking), October 1954, pp. 10-13.

Davis, W. M. "Geomorphology of Western Tibet." *Geographical Review* 21 (April 1931): 321.

De Terra, H., and Hutchinson, G. E. "Evidence of Recent

Climatic Changes Shown by Tibetan Highland Lakes." *Geographical Journal* 84 (October 1934): 311-20.

Futterer, C. "Geographische Skizze von Nordost-Tibet." *Mittheilungen aus J. Perthas geographischer Anstalt Erganzungsheft* 143 (1903): 1-66.

"Hedin's Data on Tibet Revised by Satellite Photos." *New York Times*, February 13, 1969, p. 14.

Hsu Chi-ch'uan and Yang Te-yung. "Clay Mineral Composition and Variations of Some Major Soils in Tibetan Plateau." *T'u Jang Hsueh Pao* [Journal of Pedology] (Peking), 12, no. 3 (1964): 275-85.

Huntington, Ellsworth. "Pangong, a Glacial Lake in the Tibetan Plateau." *Journal of Geology* 14, no. 7 (October/November 1906): 599-617.

Kaulback, Ronald. "Journey in the Salween and Tsangpo Basins, Southeast Tibet." *Geographical Journal* 91 (February 1938): 97-122.

Trinkler, Emil. "The Ice-Age on the Tibetan Plateau and in Adjacent Regions." *Geographical Journal* 75 (1930): 225-32.

Vaurie, Charles. *Tibet and Its Birds*. London: Witherby, 1972. [Geography and natural regions of Tibet are discussed; contains good illustrations of the Tibetan landscape.]

Vegetation of Central Tibet. Compiled by Tibet Comprehensive Observation Team, Chinese Academy of Sciences. Peking: Science Publishers, 1966. [Includes list of references.]

Ward, F. K. "Botanical and Geographical Explorations in Tibet, 1935." *Geographical Journal* 88 (November 1936): 385-413.

————. *The Mystery Rivers of Tibet*. London: Seeley, 1923.

————. A *Plant Hunter in Tibet*. London: Jonathan Cape, 1934.

————. *The Riddle of the Tsangpo Gorges*. London: Arnold, 1926.

Yusov, B. V. *Tibet: fiziko-geograficheskaya Kharakteristika*. Moscow, 1958. [Translated from Russian by the Joint Publications Research Service, U.S. Department of Commerce, Washington, D.C., and published as *Physical Geography of Tibet* (1959).]

People

Ahmad Shah. *Pictures of Tibetan Life*. Benares: Lazarus, 1906.

Chapman, F. S. "Lhasa in 1937." *Geographical Journal* 91 (June 1938): 497-507.

————. *Lhasa, the Holy City*. Freeport, N.Y.: Books for Libraries Press, 1972. [Reprint of 1940 edition.]

Chopra, M. K. "Red China Colonizes Tibet." *Military Review* 46 (July 1966): 52-60.

Ekvall, Robert B. "Nomads of Tibet: A Chinese Dilemma." *Current Scene* (Hong Kong), 1, no. 13 (September 23, 1961).

Freeberne, Michael. "Changing Population Characteristics in Tibet, 1959–1965." *Population Studies* 19 (March 1966): 317-20.

Hazelhurst, Peter. "China Tries to End Tibetan Exodus." *Times* (London), October 20, 1967, p. 7.

India, Army, Intelligence Branch. *Diary of a Journey across Tibet*, by H. Bower. Calcutta: Superintendent of Government Printing, 1893.

Krull, Germaine. *Tibetans in India*. Bombay: Allied Publishers, 1968.

Maraini, F. "Religion and People in Tibet." *Geographical Magazine* 24 (July 1951): 241-43.

Narayana Rao, Shanti. "Tibetan Refugees: Working Hard to Build a New Life." *Indian Express*, December 17, 1972, p. 8.

Olschak, Blanche Christine. *Tibet: Erde der Gotter*. Zurich: Rascher, 1960. [Map, illustrations.]

————. "Tibetans in Migration." *International Migration* 5 (1967): 187-95.

Orleans, Leo A. "A Note on Tibet's Population." *China Quarterly* 27 (July–September 1966): 120-22.

Ott-Marti, Anna Elisabeth. *Tibeter in der Schweiz: Kulturelle Verhaltensweisen im Wandel*. Erlenbach, Zurich: Eugen Rentsch, 1971.

Patterson, George N. *God's Fool*. London: Faber and Faber, 1959. [Author's experiences as a missionary in Tibet.]

Snellgrove, David L. "For a Sociology of Tibetan Speaking Regions." *Central Asiatic Review*, September 1966, pp. 199-219.

Taring, Richen Dalma. *Daughter of Tibet*. London: Murray, 1970. [Description of Tibetan family life and customs by a well-known Tibetan lady in exile since 1959 who is now managing the Homes for Tibetan Children in Mussoine, India.]

"Tibet, High Land of Monk and Nomad." *Journal of Asian Studies* 27 (May 1968): 603-08.

Tibetans in Exile, 1959–1969: A Report on Ten Years of Rehabilitation in India. Compiled by the Office of H. H. the Dalai Lama, Dharmsala, 1969.

White, J. C. *Tibet and Lhasa*. 2 vols. Calcutta: Johnston and Hoffman, 1908. [Photographs.]

Religion and Culture

Banerjee, Ankul Chandra. "Indo-Tibetan Cultural Relations." In *India's Contribution to World Thought and Culture*, ed. Lokesh Chandra; Madras: Vivekananda Rock Memorial Committee, 1970, pp. 393-400.

Conze, Edward. *Buddhism: Its Essence and Development*. Oxford: Cassirer, 1951; New York: Harper, 1959.

Dalai Lama XIV. "India: The Home of Tibetan Learning." In *India's Contribution to World Thought and Culture*, ed. Lokesh Chandra; Madras: Vivekananda Rock Memorial Committee, 1970, pp. 389-92.

David-Neel, Alexandra. *Magic and Mystery in Tibet*. New York: Dover Publications, 1971.

Duncon, Marion H. *Customs and Superstitions of Tibetans*. London: Mitre Press, 1964.

Ekvall, Robert B. *Religious Observances in Tibet*. Chicago: University of Chicago Press, 1964.

Eliade, Mircea. *Shamanism*. London: Routledge, 1964.

Guenther, H. V., trans. *Treasures on the Tibetan Middle Way*. Berkeley: Shambala Publications, 1971. [A newly revised edition of *Tibetan Buddhism without Mystification*.]

Hoffman, Helmut. *The Religions of Tibet*. London: Kegan Paul, 1961.

Lukas, J. Anthony. "Tibetans Accuse Chinese of Desecrating Temple." *New York Times*, February 7, 1967, p. 10.

Nebesky-Wojkowitz, René de. *Oracles and Demons of Tibet: The Cult and Iconography of the Tibetan Protective Deities*. The Hague and London: Mouton, 1956.

Sierksma, Fokke. *Tibet's Terrifying Deities: Sex and Aggression in Religious Acculturation*. Rutland, Vt.: G. E. Tuttle, 1966.

Sinha, Nirmal Chandra. *Prolegomena to Lamaist Polity*. Calcutta: F. K. L. Mukhopadhyay, 1969. [Discusses the concepts of Refuge and Incarnation in the constitutional history of Tibet.]

Tucci, Giuseppe. *Tibetan Painted Scrolls*. 2 vols. Rome: Libreria dello Stato, 1949. [This is the authoritative, comprehensive work on religion, literature, and history, despite its misleading title.]

Waddell, L. A. *The Buddhism of Tibet, or Lamaism*, 2nd ed. New York: Harper, 1973.

Economy

Carrasco, Pedro. *Land and Polity in Tibet*. Seattle: University of Washington Press, 1959.

Chang Kuo-hua. "Tibet Reaps a Bumper Harvest after Democratic Reform." *Hung-ch'i* [Red Flag, Peking], no. 23 (December 1, 1960): 32-36.

Chang Po-chun. "First Highways to Tibet." *China Reconstructs* (Peking), 4, no. 5 (May 1955): 2-5.

"Chinese Scientists Carry Forward Comprehensive Survey on Chinghai-Tibet Plateau." *Economic Reporter* (English Supplement), no. 2 (April-June 1975): 36-38.

Downs, James F. "Livestock, Production, and Social Mobility in High Altitude Tibet." *American Anthropologist* 66, no. 5 (October 1964): 1115-19.

"Facts about Tibet." *Peking Review* 8, no. 38 (September 17, 1965): 28-29.

"Glimpses of Tibet Today." *Peking Review* 8, no. 37 (September 10, 1965): 26; no. 38 (September 17, 1965): 27.

Jih-nung. "Highways on the 'Roof of the World.'" *China Reconstructs* 14, no. 9 (September 1965): 24-26.

Jones, P. H. M. "Tibet's Emerging Economy." *Far Eastern Economic Review* 31, no. 7 (February 16, 1961): 288-91.

Kingdom-Ward, F. "Tibet as a Grazing Land." *Geographical Journal* 110 (1947): 60-75.

Kuo Li-Hua. "Medical Teams in Tibet." *China Reconstructs* 24, no. 5 (May 1975): 44-46.

"Large-Scale Surveys on the Roof of the World." *Eastern Horizon* 7 (January 1968): 42-44.

Li Teh-shen. "A Visit to a Tibetan Farm Co-op." *Peking Review* 2 (June 23, 1959): 15-16.

Macdonald, David. *Tibet.* Oxford Pamphlets on Indian Affairs, no. 30. Bombay: Oxford University Press, 1945.

Notes on Tibetan Trade. Compiled by William Stirling Hamilton. Lahore: Government of Punjab, 1910.

Palmieri, Richard P. "The Domestication, Exploitation, and Social Functions of the Yak in Tibet and Adjoining Areas." *Proceedings of the Association of American Geographers* 4 (1972): 80-83.

Panchen Erdeni. "Tibet in 1960." *Peking Review* 4, no. 2 (January 13, 1961): 15-22.

Pan Kuo-ting. "Flight to Lhasa." In *China in Transition* (Peking, 1957), pp. 178-83.

"Tibet: Rural Postal Service." *Peking Review* 18, no. 18 (May 2, 1975): 30-31.

"Tibet Today." *Peking Review* 7, no. 51 (December 18, 1964): 14-16.

"Transport Fighters on the 'Roof of the World.'" *China Pictorial*, no. 12 (1968): 32-36.

Political Setting

Alexandrowicz-Alexander, Charles H. "The Legal Position of Tibet." *American Journal of International Law* 48, no. 2 (April 1954): 265-74.

Bradsher, Henry S. "Tibet Struggles to Survive." *Foreign Affairs* 47, no. 4 (July 1969): 750-62.

Caroe, Sir Olaf. "Tibet: The End of an Era." *Royal Central Asian Journal* 47 (January 1960): 22-34.

Chandrasekharan, M. "The Question of Tibet in the United Nations." *Indian Journal of International Law* 6, no. 1 (January 1966): 32-44.

Chang Kuo-hua. "A New Tibet Is Arising." *People's China* (Peking), 10 (May 16, 1953): 7-11.

Chowdhury, J. N. "British Contributions to the Confusion of Tibet's Status." *Quest*, no. 54 (July-September 1967): 32-38.

Clubb, O. E. "Tibet Strategic Position." *Eastern World* 10 (December 1956): 18-19.

"Communism in Tibet." *China News Analysis* (Hong Kong), no. 378 (June 30, 1961).

Dalai Lama XIV. "Future of Tibetans." *Indian Review* 66 (February/March 1967): 64-65.

Dean, V. M. "The Impact of Tibet." *Foreign Policy Bulletin* 38 (May 1, 1959): 124, 127-28.

Gittings, John. "Sound and Fury in Tibet." *Far Eastern Economic Review* 61 (September 12, 1968): 516-19.

Gopal, Ram. *India-China-Tibet Triangle.* Lucknow: Pustak Kendra, 1964.

Gould, Sir Basil. "Tibet and Her Neighbours." *International Affairs* 26 (January 1950): 71-76.

Government of H. H. the Dalai Lama. *The International Position of Tibet.* Delhi: Bureau of H. H. the Dalai Lama, 1959.

Henze, P. B. "The Strategic Significance of Recent Events in Tibet." *Royal Central Asian Society Journal* 40 (April 1953): 163-73.

International Commission of Jurists, Legal Inquiry Committee on Tibet. *Tibet and the Chinese People's Republic.* Geneva, 1960. [Report.]

Li Tieh-tseng. "The Legal Position of Tibet." *American Journal of International Law* 50 (April 1956): 394-404.

————. *Tibet: Today and Yesterday.* New York: Bookman Associates, 1960.

Lockhart, Robert B. "Tibet in the New Chinese Empire." *United Asia* 18, no. 4 (July/August 1966): 176-78.

Mellor, Roy. "The Changing Geographical Value of Tibet." *Scottish Geographical Magazine* 75, no. 2 (September 1959): 113-15.

Nag, B. C. "Chinese Troop Concentration in Tibet." *Swarajya* (Delhi), 10, no. 42 (April 16, 1966): 4.

Niemi, M. L. "Recent Trends in Chinese Communist Control of Tibet." *Far Eastern Survey* 27 (July 1958): 104-07.

Patterson, G. N. "Recent Chinese Policies in Tibet." *China Quarterly* 12 (October-December 1962): 191-202.

Peissel, Michael. *Cavaliers of Kham: The Secret War in Tibet.* London: Heinemann, 1972.

Pringsheim, K. "The Conflict in Tibet." *Contemporary China* 4 (1959–1960): 70-86.

Rahul, Ram. *The Government and Politics of Tibet.* Delhi: Vikas Publications, 1969.

————. "The Role of Lamas in Central Asian Politics." *Central Asiatic Journal* 12, no. 3 (1969): 209-27.

Rubin, Alfred P. "The Position of Tibet in International Law." *China Quarterly* 18 (September 1968): 110-54.

Walsh, E. H. C. *The Coinage of Tibet.* Calcutta: Baptist Mission Press, 1907.

Wylie, Turrell V. "Tibetan Passports: Their Function and Significance." *Central Asiatic Journal* 12, no. 2 (1968): 149-52.

Historical Background and Tibetan Uprising

"Arrival of the Reincarnated Buddha at Lhasa." *Nature* 144 (November 11, 1939): 826.

Bacot, Jacques. *Introduction à l'histoire du Tibet.* Paris: Société Asiatique, 1962. [Map, illustrations.]

Concerning the Question of Tibet. Peking: Foreign Languages Press, 1959.

Dhyani, S. N. *Contemporary Tibet: Its Status in International Law.* Lucknow: Capital Law House, 1961.

Elwin, Verrier. "The Dalai Lama Comes to India." *Geographical Magazine* 32, no. 4 (1959): 161-69.

Haarh, Erik. *The Yar-lun Dynasty: A Study with Particular Regard to the Contributions by Myths and Legends to the History of Ancient Tibet and the Origin and Nature of Its Kings.* Copenhagen: Gad, 1969.

Jain, G. L. "India and the Tibetan Revolt." *Atlantic Monthly* 204 (December 1959): 85-88.

Kolmas, Josef. *Tibet and Imperial China: A Survey of Sino-Tibetan Relations up to the End of the Manchu Dynasty in 1912.* Canberra: Centre of Oriental Studies, Australian National University, 1967.

Mehra, Parshotam. *The Younghusband Expedition: An Interpretation.* Bombay: Asia Publishing Co., 1968.

Nag, B. C. "Tibetans Rise in Revolt Again." *Swarajya* (Delhi), 11, no. 26 (December 24, 1966): 17-18.

Norbu, Thubten Jigme, and Turnbull, Colin M. *Tibet: An Account of the History, the Religion, and the People of Tibet.* New York: Simon and Schuster, 1969.

Patterson, George N. *A Fool at Forty.* Waco, Texas: Word Books, 1970.

Petech, L. *China and Tibet in the Early 18th Century: History of the Establishment of the Chinese Protectorate in Tibet.* Leiden: E. J. Brill, 1950.

"Reincarnation of a Dalai Lama." *Nature* 144 (November 4, 1939): 779.

Richardson, H. E. *Tibet: Past and Present.* Saskatoon: University of Saskatchewan, 1967.

"Signs of Revolt in Tibet." *Times* (London), December 14, 1964, p. 9.

Strong, Anna Louise. *When Serfs Stood Up in Tibet: A Report.* Peking: New World Press, 1960.

Tu, Hêng-chih. *A Study of the Treaties and Agreements Relating to Tibet: A Documentary History of the International Relations of Tibet.* Taichung, Taiwan: Tunghai University, 1971.

Valiakhmetov, Gali M. *State and Administrative Organs of Tibet.* New York: U.S. Joint Publication Research Service, 1959.

"While Europe Prepares for War, Pious Tibet Searches for the Child Ruler." *China Weekly Review* 81 (July 10, 1937): 201-02.

Communist Occupation

Afro-Asian Convention on Tibet and against Colonialism in Asia and Africa. *Truth about Tibet.* New Delhi: Preparatory Bureau, Afro-Asian Convention on Tibet and against Colonialism in Asia and Africa, 1960.

Ahmad, Zahiruddin. *China and Tibet, 1708–1959: A Resume of Facts.* London: Royal Institute of International Affairs, 1960.

Allman, T. D. "Red Star over Shangri-la." *Far Eastern Economic Review* 83, no. 6 (February 11, 1974): 26-29.

Bambi, R. P. *The Crusaders of Tibet.* Dalhousie, Himachal Pradesh: Khampa Pocket Books, 1970.

"Bright Sunshine in Tibet." *China Reconstructs* (Peking), 17, no. 12 (December 1968): 21-27. [An account of the Cultural Revolution in Tibet.]

Chao Chia-lieh. "Showing the New Face of Tibet." *China Reconstructs,* no. 2 (February 1961): 9-13.

"Chinese May be Loosening their Grip on Tibet." *Economist* 249 (October 6, 1973): 37-38.

"Diplomacy and the Dalai Lama." *Far Eastern Economic Review* 83, no. 11 (March 18, 1974): 22.

Ford, Robert Webster. *Captured in Tibet.* London: George G. Harrap, 1957. [An account of the author's experiences

during and after the Chinese invasion of Tibet, 1950.]

Gelder, Stuart, and Gelder, Roma. "The Truth about Tibet." *Eastern Horizon*, August 1963, pp. 9-25; September 1963, pp. 16-31; October 1963, pp. 16-26.

Gilbert, Rodney Yonkers. *Genocide in Tibet: A Study in Communist Aggression.* New York: American-Asian Educational Exchange, 1959.

Ginsburgs, G. and Mathos, M. "Communist China's Impact on Tibet: The First Decade." *Far Eastern Survey* 29 (July 1960): 102-09; (August 1960): 120-24.

Hutheesing, G. P., ed. *Tibet Fights for Freedom: The Story of the March 1959 Uprising as Recorded in Documents, Despatches, Eye-witness Accounts and World-wide Reactions.* With a foreword by the Dalai Lama. Bombay: Published for the Indian Committee for Cultural Freedom by Orient Longmans, 1961.

Institute of National Affairs, Delhi. *Dalai Lama and India: Indian Public and Prime Minister on Tibetan Crisis.* Ed. Rajeswara Rau. New Delhi: Hind Book House, 1959.

International Studies 10 (April 1969). [Special number devoted entirely to papers on Tibet.]

Jones, P. H. M. "Respite for Tibet." *Far Eastern Economic Review* 32, no. 8 (May 25, 1961): 365-67.

————. "Tibet and the New Order." *Far Eastern Economic Review* 31, no. 9 (March 2, 1961): 356, 360-62.

————. "Tibet Comes into Line." *Far Eastern Economic Review* 34, no. 13 (December 28, 1961): 589-91.

Kolb, Albert. "Tibet: The Chinese Impact on a Theocratic State." In idem, *East Asia: China, Japan, Korea, Vietnam; Geography of a Cultural Region.* Trans. C. A. M. Sym. London: Methuen, 1971.

"Persecution of Tibetans by Chinese Occupation Army." *Times* (London), January 13, 1965, p. 9.

"Renewed Unrest Reported in Tibet." *New York Times,* November 16, 1969, p. 6.

Rūfāil, Wadi. *The Tibetan Revolt.* New York: U. S. Joint Publications Research Service, 1959.

Sen, Chanakya. *Tibet Disappears: A Documentary History of Tibet's International Status, the Great Rebellion and Its Aftermath.* New York: Asia Publishing House, 1960.

Senanayake, Ratne D. *Inside Story of Tibet.* Colombo: Afro-Asian Writer's Bureau, 1967.

"The Tibetan Plateau under the Sunlight of Mao Tse-tung's Thought." *China Pictorial,* no. 11 (1968): 16-21.

Thubtob, Ngawang. *Tibet Today.* Delhi: Bureau of H. H. the Dalai Lama, n.d.

"U.S. Affirms Belief in Principle of Self-determination for Tibet." [Messages by C. A. Herter and the Dalai Lama.] *U.S. Department of State Bulletin* 42 (March 21, 1960): 443.

"U.S. Expresses Concern at the Actions of Chinese Communists in Tibet." [Statement, March 26, 1959, by C. A. Herter.] *U.S. Department of State Bulletin* 40 (April 13, 1959): 514-15.

"Violence Raging in Tibet." *Times* (London), September 27, 1967, p. 1.

Wiederkehr, Emil, ed. *S.O.S. Tibet: Documents et Rapports Sur l'Oppression du Tibet et la Menace Mondial de la Chine Communiste.* Berne: Comité d'Aide aux Victimes du Communisme, 1960.

Travel and Exploration

Only items of substantial merit from the viewpoint of geography are included here.

Bell, Sir Charles. *Index to Cards.* 2 vols. London: British Museum. 1938 [A subject index to the "Diary" and "Notebooks" on Tibet, Bhutan, Sikkim and the Chumbi Valley by Sir C. A. Bell and to works on Tibet by various authors.]

David-Neel, Louise Alexandra Eugenie Marie. *My Journey to Lhasa.* Harmondsworth, New York: Allen Lane, 1940.

Hedin, Sven Anders. *Central Asia and Tibet: Towards the Holy City of Lassa.* New York: Greenwood Press, 1969. [Reprint of 1903 edition.]

Kemp, E. G. "An Artist's Impression of Western Tibet and Turkestan." *Proceedings of the Central Asian Society, 1913.* Pp. 1-16.

Macdonald, A. *Through the Heart of Tibet.* Glasgow: Blackie and Son, 1910.

Macdonald, David. *Touring in Sikkim and Tibet.* Calcutta: Thacker and Spink, 1943.

McGovern, William Montgomery. *To Lhasa in Disguise: A Secret Expedition through Mysterious Tibet.* New York: Century, 1924.

Markham, Clements Robert, ed. *Narratives of the Mission of George Bogle to Tibet and of the Journey of Thomas Manning to Lhasa.* 2nd ed. New Delhi: Manjusri, 1971.

Pranavananda, Swami. *Exploration in Tibet.* Calcutta: University of Calcutta, 1939.

Teichman, E. *Travels of a Consular Officer in Eastern Tibet.* Cambridge: Cambridge University Press, 1922.

Tucci, Giuseppe. *Trans-Himalaya.* Paris: Nagel, 1973.

Warwick, Alan Ross. *With Younghusband in Tibet.* Adventures in Geography Series. London: F. Mellor, 1962.

Miscellaneous Documents

India, Lok Sabha [House of the People]. *Debates,* 5(4) (November 20, 1950), cols. 155-56, Indian Prime Minister Nehru's statement on Indo-Tibetan boundary situation; 6(17) (December 6, 1950): cols. 1266-67, Nehru on advance of Chinese forces into Tibet; 6(18) (December 7, 1950), cols. 1383-84, Nehru on situation in Tibet; 28(32) (March 23, 1959), cols. 1706-10, and 28(32) (March 30, 1959), cols. 8514-26, Nehru's statement to the House on situation in Tibet; 31(64) (May 8, 1959), cols. 15865-940, debate on the situation in Tibet; 32(4) (August 6, 1959), cols. 930-34, Nehru's statement in the House on difficulties facing the Indian traders in Tibet; 33(16) (August 24, 1959), cols. 7074-77, on the risks to Indian pilgrims in visiting Tibet.

————. Resolution regarding Tibet, June 30, 1967. *Debates,* n.s. 5(29), cols. 8883-922.

————. Resolutions regarding Tibet, July 14, 1967. *Debates,* n.s. 6(39), cols. 11958-12032.

India Office Library, London. Political and Secret Memoranda, 1919, J. E. Shuckburgh, Tibet.

————. Bell Papers.

United Nations, General Assembly. Official Records. 5th Session, Annexes, vol. 1 (1950): 16-18. Memorandum (Document A/1534) from the chairman of the delegation of El Salvador to the president of the General Assembly about invasion of Tibet by foreign forces; memorandum (Document A/1549) of Tibetan delegation to the Secretary General about invasion of Tibet by China.

————. Official Records. 5th Session, General Committee, 73rd meeting, November 24, 1950, pp. 17-20. Debate on "Invasion of Tibet by foreign forces."

————. Official Records. 14th Session, Plenary Meetings, (1959), 831st to 834th Plenary Meetings, October 20-21, 1959, pp. 469-530. Debate on the question of Tibet.

————. Official Records. 20th Session, Plenary Meetings, vol. 3 (1965), 1394th Plenary Meeting, December 14, 1965, pp. 1-10. Debate on the question of Tibet.

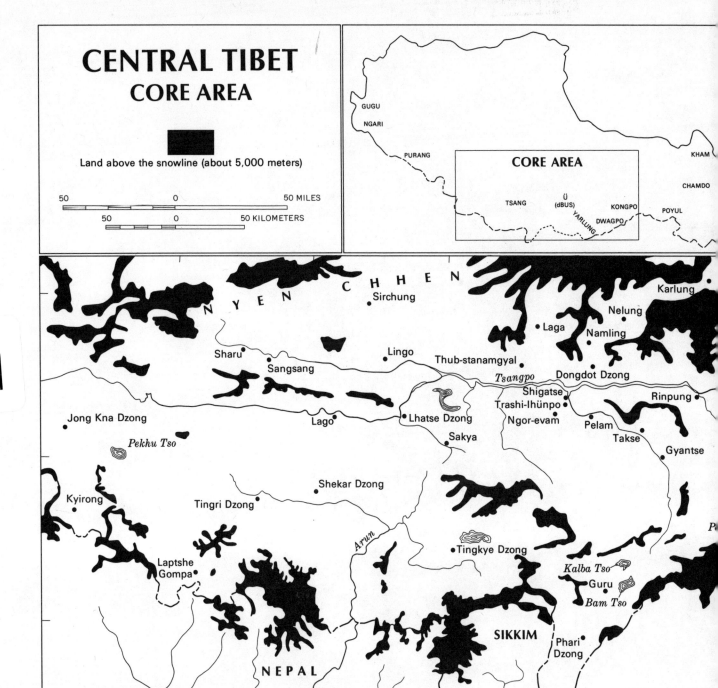

CENTRAL TIBET
CORE AREA

Land above the snowline (about 5,000 meters)

50   0   50 MILES

50   0   50 KILOMETERS

CORE AREA

GUGU

NGARI

PURANG

TSANG   Ü
(dBUS)   KONGPO

YARLUNG   DWAGPO

KHAM

CHAMDO

POYUL

N Y E N   C H H E N

Sirchung

Karlung

Nelung

Laga   Namling

Sharu   Lingo

Sangsang   Thub-stanamgyal   Dongdot Dzong

Tsangpo

Shigatse   Rinpung

Trashi-lhünpo

Jong Kna Dzong   Lago   Lhatse Dzong   Ngor-evam   Pelam

Takse

Sakya   Gyantse

Pekhu Tso

Shekar Dzong

Kyirong   Tingri Dzong

Arun   Tingkye Dzong

Kalba Tso

Laptshe
Gompa   Guru

Bam Tso

SIKKIM   Phari
Dzong

N E P A L

86°   87°   88°   89°   90